MICROWAVE
made easy

MICROWAVE
made easy

COURAGE
BOOKS
AN IMPRINT OF
RUNNING PRESS
PHILADELPHIA, PENNSYLVANIA

Editor: Diana Craig
Designer: Gordon Robertson
Production: Dennis Hovell

© Marshall Cavendish Limited 1986

Canadian representatives: General Publishing Co Ltd.,
30 Lesmill Road. Don Mills, Ontario M3B 2T6
9 8 7 6 5 4 3 2 1
Digit on the right indicates the number of this printing.

Cataloging in Publication data

MICROWAVE MADE EASY
Compiled by Marshall Cavendish
Includes index.
1.   Microwave Cookery, I. Cavendish, Marshall.
TX832.M534   1986   641.5′682   86–11459
ISBN   0–89471–484–8 cloth
Printed and bound in Italy by L.E.G.O. S.p.a. Vicenza

This book can be ordered by mail from the publisher.
Please include $1.00 for postage and handling. But try your
bookstore first! Published by Courage Books, an imprint of
Running Press Book Publishers, 125 South 22nd Street, Philadelphia
PA 19103

C·O·N·T·E·N·T·S

I·N·T·R·O·D·U·C·T·I·O·N

Microwave ovens are becoming an increasingly familiar sight in today's kitchens as more and more people discover the enormous benefits to be gained from microwave cookery. Whether you cook for a family or just for one, the greatest benefits of all are savings both of time and energy.

A microwave oven uses less electricity simply because it cooks food in so much less time than a conventional oven and because all energy is used on the food – none is wasted on heating up plates or on the oven itself. Whole meals may be cooked in minutes; a plate of food can be warmed through without waiting for the oven to heat up; baked potatoes and casseroles which previously needed hours in the oven can be ready in a fraction of the time; and you don't even need to boil the kettle to make a cup of coffee.

Cooking in a microwave oven is not only fast and economical, but it is also 'healthy'. Many foods benefit from faster cooking, especially vegetables which may be cooked so quickly, and in such a small amount of water, that they retain most of their nutritional value.

One of the best things about microwave ovens is that their use need not be limited to cooking food. If you own a freezer, a microwave oven is an ideal companion because it can thaw food in minutes. You no longer need to panic if you've forgotten to take the chicken out of the freezer, or if the dough is still rock-solid five minutes before you want to start baking. Just put them in the microwave, switch to 'low' or 'defrost' and the food will be ready for use in minutes. Your microwave will also come in handy when you need to soften butter for sandwiches or for mixing a cake, or to melt chocolate for a sauce or cake frosting.

Once you have a microwave oven installed in your kitchen, and you become familiar and confident with its use, you'll discover the countless ways it can make your life easier. This book is designed to do just that – to make microwave cookery easy so that you can gain the confidence to reap all its benefits.

L·E·A·R·N·I·N·G T·H·E B·A·S·I·C·S

Understanding the basics makes microwave cookery easy.
Here you will find all you need to know –
how the oven works, what cookware to use
and how to cook, warm up or thaw food in your microwave oven.

There are so many microwave ovens on the market today that choosing one can seem a daunting prospect. The one you choose will, of course, depend on your own needs and the amount of money you want to spend. Once you have made a choice, read the manufacturer's handbook very carefully. It will tell you all you need to know about your new oven, including where best to place it, its power output, and how to look after it.

GETTING TO KNOW YOUR MICROWAVE OVEN
A basic understanding of how microwave ovens work, and how to look after them, is the first step towards successful cookery.

Looking after your oven
All microwave ovens are remarkably easy to keep clean, but there are a few basic points to remember. The inside of the oven needs only a wipe with a damp cloth after each use – never use anything that may scratch the metal lining of the oven, such as scouring pads or cleansing powder. If spatters or food spills do occur, clean them up immediately,

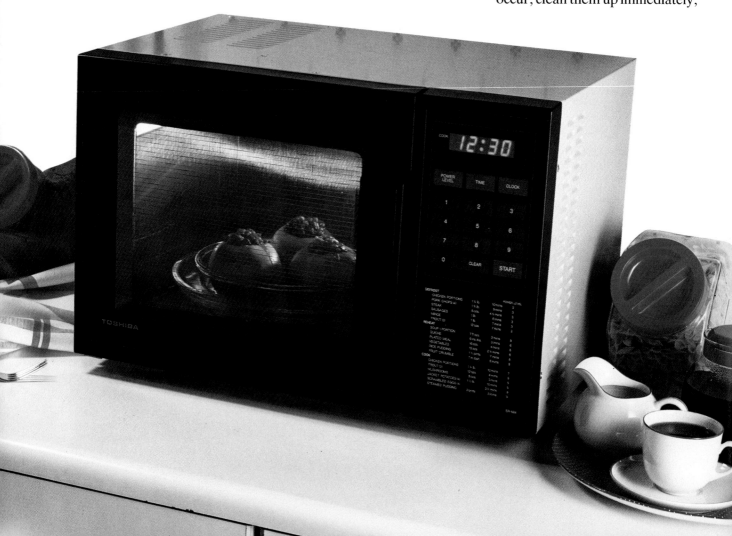

especially if particles of food gather around the door seals as these must be kept clear.

The oven can easily be damaged if it is turned on when there is nothing inside it. To avoid this, keep a cup or small bowl of water in the oven in case it is accidentally turned on.

Power outputs

The power output of microwave ovens varies from one model to another. Most domestic models range from 500-700 watts. The power output determines how quickly your oven will work. A 500-watt oven will cook, thaw or reheat food more slowly than a 600-watt oven. Ovens with a high wattage output usually have variable controls. If you have an oven with a low wattage output, the choice may be limited to one or two settings. A more sophisticated microwave oven may have a wide range of variable settings, and may also include a warming facility and built-in browning element (which utilizes conventional radiant heat).

How microwave cookery works

In order to cook, thaw or heat food, microwave ovens convert normal electricity into microwave energy which is directed into the oven compartment. To ensure that the microwaves are distributed evenly, a paddle or stirrer blade is built into the roof of the oven and this is constantly turning whenever the oven is in operation. The microwaves are unable to escape through the tough metal casing or tight-fitting door and the metal lining of the oven continually reflects the microwaves back on to the contents of the oven. All microwave ovens have a built-in safety device that automatically switches off the oven the instant the door is opened, and the microwaves disappear as soon as the power is turned off.

Microwaves are similar to radio waves but are much shorter, hence their name. The waves cannot pass through metal, so within the metal-lined oven they bounce backward and forward, aiming their energy at whatever is in the oven. Microwaves are absorbed by particles of water and are attracted to the water particles in food. They cause the particles to vibrate, generating heat by friction. It is this heat that cooks the food. As microwaves are so short, they can only penetrate food to a depth of $1\frac{1}{2}$-2 inches but the heat created passes right into the food by means of conduction so that thicker items of food may be cooked right through.

WHAT COOKWARE TO USE

One of the most surprising things about microwave cooking is that although water may boil, and food gets hot enough to cook, containers used rarely become too hot to lift out of the oven without a cloth. Microwaves pass straight through to the food, leaving containers and oven cool. Natural transfer of heat from food to dish will occur, however,

B·A·S·I·C K·N·O·W-H·O·W

Ovenproof glass baking dishes of all shapes and sizes may be used in a microwave oven. Use heat-resistant glass measuring cups for making sauces, and small mixing bowls for cooking desserts, melting gelatin or warming up food.

Glass-ceramic casseroles and saucepans are also ideal for microwave cookery. They may be used under a browner or stay-hot element or in a conventional oven, if food needs to be kept hot before serving. Many dishes are also attractive enough to serve in.

and some containers will get hotter than others, so you should always take care. Any steam produced during cooking will, of course, be as hot as it always is, so be careful when lifting lids.

As containers do not get very hot, it is possible to use a surprising variety of cookware in a microwave oven. The most important thing to remember, of course, is not to use anything metal, including baking pans and sheets of any sort, foil dishes, foil-lined convenience food containers, and foil coverings unless your handbook specifically states that metal may be used. Even so, follow the manufacturer's directions closely and do not allow any

metal to come in contact with the sides of the oven.

If you do use metal in an oven not designed for it, not only will the microwaves be unable to penetrate the food, but you are also likely to damage the lining of your oven. Watch out for metal trim on china or glass, detachable handles, screws in lids, and glassware made from lead crystal, none of which should be used in the oven.

You've only got to look around your kitchen to discover how many things can be used in the oven, however, and some of them may surprise you. You'll find you can save on the dish washing by mixing and cooking

in the same bowl, and you'll be able to take something out of the freezer, thaw and reheat it in the microwave, and put it straight on the table using just one dish.

China, pottery and glass
China and pottery are both ideal for microwave cookery, although food may take slightly longer to cook in a pottery container. You must not use any china that has a metal trim, however.

Oven-to-table and ceramic glass cookware may also be used, as can any glass dish that is strong enough to withstand high temperatures.

If in any doubt as to the suitability of a dish, try the following test. Stand a glass cup containing 1 cup water in the dish to be tested. Microwave at 100% (high) for 1 minute. If the dish feels cool, and the water is hot, the dish is safe to use for microwave cooking.

Paper and plastic
Surprisingly, it is perfectly safe to use paper and plastic in a microwave oven except, of course, in conjunction with a browner or warming element. Use paper plates and cups for reheating, not for cooking, and use sheets of absorbent kitchen paper for covering food or for standing food on. Do not use recycled paper products – they may contain impurities which might cause arcing. Waxed paper and cardboard containers and plastic supermarket cartons should only be used when thawing or reheating food as they may melt if they get too hot.

Food may be cooked in oven roasting bags and boil-in pouches as long as they are pierced to allow steam to escape. Seal bags with rubber bands or string rather than with the metal twist-ties provided. Do not use ordinary plastic bags in a microwave as they will melt.

B·A·S·I·C K·N·O·W-H·O·W

Non-porous pottery dishes may be used in a microwave oven. Use mugs for making coffee, plates for reheating meals, and casseroles for cooking and serving.

China plates and dishes of all sorts are microwave-safe as long as they have no metal trim. Flan and china soufflé molds, gratin dishes and custard cups may all be used.

Plastic wrap is perfect for covering food to be cooked in a microwave oven.

Wood and basketware

Wooden boards may be used when reheating bread, and rolls may be warmed in a basket, ready for serving. If used too often, however, wood and basketware might dry out and crack.

Microwave cookware

If you cannot find the ideal dish in your kitchen, more and more cookware, specially designed for microwave cookery, is available in the stores. The dishes range from large casserole containers to single-meal divided plates and cake-baking dishes.

Shape and size of cookware

The size of container used to thaw, reheat or cook food in the microwave is very important. If a dish is too small, food may bubble over; if it is too large, food could dry out.

Round or oval-shaped dishes give the best results. Dishes with corners can cause uneven cooking as food receives twice as much microwave energy in the corners. However, if you do wish to use a square or rectangular dish, it may be possible to shield the food in the corners with small pieces of foil (see 'Shielding'). Choose straight-sided containers if possible and remember that a shallow dish of food will cook more quickly than a full, deep one.

Non-metallic ring molds are ideal for cakes and other foods which cannot be stirred during cooking. They allow the microwaves to penetrate from the center as well as from the outside, resulting in quicker, more even cooking.

Pre-packaged frozen meals

It's even possible these days to avoid dish washing altogether as you can buy certain frozen foods and some complete meals ready-packaged in microproof plastic or cardboard containers which can be put straight in your microwave oven. You'll find detailed directions for cooking on each package so all you need to do for a quick lunch or supper is to put the package in the microwave for the stated time, unwrap and transfer to a warmed plate, if wished, or eat your meal straight out of the specially designed container.

BASIC TECHNIQUES

Shielding

It is sometimes necessary to protect thin pieces of food from overcooking, for example, the ends of chicken or lamb bones or the tail end of a fish. As microwaves will not pass through metal, thin strips of foil may be used for this 'shielding' purpose for part of the cooking time. Before using this technique, however, check in your oven handbook as some manufacturers recommend avoiding use of even small amounts of foil.

Foil used for shielding should be kept as smooth as possible and used only in a single layer. It should never be allowed to come in contact with any part of the interior of the oven.

Another effective way of shielding food from microwaves in order to prevent overcooking is to mask it with a generous portion of sauce. This method also helps to prevent foods drying out when reheating.

Standing time

Much more than with conventional cooking, food continues to cook when it is taken out of a microwave oven. Food should therefore be taken out of the oven before it is completely cooked, and left to stand until it is cooked through. Many foods will appear undercooked when first removed from the oven but will be perfectly cooked and ready to serve at the end of the specified standing time. This standing time is therefore a very important part of the microwave cooking process.

All food should be covered during standing time. It is always better to cook food in a microwave oven for the shortest time suggested, let it stand, then test to see if it is cooked. It is then possible to put it back in the oven for a minute or two if it is not cooked to your liking. Once overcooked, however, nothing can be done about it.

Turning and stirring

It is necessary to turn food during cooking to ensure even distribution of microwaves. Some ovens have a turntable which constantly rotates the food. If your oven does not have one you will need to turn the food manually. The recipes in this book assume you are using an oven without a turntable and manual turning directions are therefore included.

Even if your oven does have a turntable, some rearrangement of food is necessary. For example, pieces of meat or poultry which stand high in the oven will need to be turned over once during cooking so that all parts receive the same amount of energy. Also, if you are cooking food in several small dishes at the same time, you will need to give each one a half turn once during cooking so that food near the center of the oven receives the same amount of energy as that on the outside. Small foods like steak or chops, and large whole vegetables, need some rearranging too, and other dishes, like soups, casseroles and sauces, will need stirring to distribute the heat evenly.

Covering

In general, foods which you would cover to cook in a conventional oven should also be covered in the microwave. As well as keeping food moist, a cover also promotes faster, more even cooking and allows for the smallest amount of liquid to be used.

When covering, remember that you must not use metal of any kind. Plastic wrap is excellent for covering food to be cooked in a microwave oven, but you need to remember to make a small slit in the wrap or to leave it partially rolled back at one side to prevent the steam creating a 'ballooning' effect. Use sheets of absorbent kitchen paper to cover foods like bacon which may spatter fat in the oven.

Browning
Food cooked in a microwave oven lacks the appetizing brown appearance that conventionally cooked food has. Food does not brown because microwave energy cooks by building up heat from the inside, and there is no outside source of heat to crisp and brown the outer surfaces of the food. If you prefer a traditional brown appearance, there are several ways of achieving this.
Savory foods may be browned using a special microwave browning dish or skillet. These have a special coating on the base which absorbs the microwaves and builds up to a temperature of 500-600° F, and they must be preheated for several minutes in the microwave (never in a conventional oven). Always follow the manufacturer's directions carefully when using a browning dish.

Some ovens now have a special built-in browning element which operates a bit like a conventional broiler. Your manufacturer's handbook will tell you how and when to use it. Of course, you can always simply put food under your conventional broiler for a few minutes after cooking to brown or crisp toppings. However, you may need to transfer

the food to a different container that can withstand the heat of the broiler. Meat or poultry may be browned in this way before microwave cooking, or, if you prefer, brown meat in a skillet first, in the usual way.

It's possible these days to buy all sorts of special microwave browning agents, but you'll also find things in your cupboard that will work just as well. For example, you could brush meat or poultry with marmalade or a mixture of melted butter and paprika, herbs or barbecue sauce, or try a mixture of equal quantities of water and soy sauce, tomato paste, ketchup or Worcestershire sauce.
Sweet foods and breads may also be browned in various ways. A plain layer cake cooked in a mic-

rowave oven looks decidedly pale and uncooked, even if the texture is perfect. This is not the case, of course, with chocolate, coffee, spiced or rich fruit cakes which will have a natural brown color, and cakes made with Graham flour and brown sugars will also be darker in appearance.

The color of a plain cake is easily improved, however, by sprinkling the surface with shredded coconut, chopped nuts, cinnamon or chopped candied fruits before cooking, or with a mixture of soft brown sugar and chopped nuts midway through the cooking time. After cooking, decorate a plain cake with a coating of plain or flavored buttercream, or a dusting of confectioners' sugar.

When cooking bread in your

B·A·S·I·C K·N·O·W-H·O·W

Covering food in a microwave may be done quickly and simply with paper towels or plastic wrap. Paper has an added advantage when covering food like bacon as it absorbs the fat quickly and prevents it spattering in the oven.

Plastic wrap should be pierced or rolled back at one edge to allow steam to escape during cooking.

Browning can be achieved in a variety of ways without using a browning dish or element or a conventional broiler. Chicken portions may be brushed with melted butter and then sprinkled with paprika, herbs, crisps, or crumbled bouillon cubes. Brushing with preserves or marmalade midway through cooking will also have a browning effect.

microwave oven, a better color will be achieved with Graham or other unbleached flours. Brushing bread with egg yolk and sprinkling with poppy, sesame or caraway seeds, cracked wheat, crushed cornflakes, dried herbs or crumbled, toasted dried onions before cooking will also help improve the color of loaves or bread rolls.

Arranging food

As microwaves only penetrate food to a depth of 1½-2 inches, food on the outside of a dish cooks more quickly than that on the inside, so it is best to place the part of the food that needs most cooking on the outside of the dish. For example, arrange chicken drumsticks on a round plate with the thin bone ends pointing toward the center and the thick fleshy parts around the outside of the plate. The microwaves will then mostly penetrate the thickest part, cooking that part thoroughly, while the thin part is cooked by the heat conducted to the center. The same applies to broccoli. The heads take less time to cook than the tough stems so place stems towards the outside of the dish where they will receive most of the microwave energy.

For more even cooking, leave some space between items of food when arranging them on a plate. If possible, place the food around the edge of the plate with nothing in the center.

Timing

For cooking, thawing and reheating basic foods, turn to pages 118-119 where a handy chart gives timing directions.

Remember that cooking time is increased if more than one item is being cooked at once. Foods with more water added also take longer to cook – another good reason for cooking foods in the minimum quantity of water.

B·A·S·I·C K·N·O·W-H·O·W

When cooking several types of vegetable together, arrange them with those that need most cooking, such as potatoes, to the outside of the dish, with those that need least cooking in the center. Pierce them gently with a fork to test whether they are cooked. Cooking times will vary according to how crisp you like your vegetables.

Density of food also affects cooking times. A medium-size baking potato will take about 4 minutes, whereas a baked apple will need only about 1½ minutes. Also, a meatloaf weighing 1 lb will need longer cooking than the same weight of ground beef.

Any spilled food in the oven can cause extra cooking time as microwaves will be attracted to that as much as to the food to be cooked.

Seasoning food

Whenever possible, add salt to food *after* it has been cooked. Foods such as meat and vegetables can become tough if cooked with salt. If you are unsure of how long food should be cooked, it is best to add salt after the standing time, in case further cooking is needed.

Thawing frozen food

The time needed for thawing food is minimal if you have a microwave oven. You can freeze, thaw and reheat or cook food in the same container, and extra portions and leftovers that have been frozen can be ready for use in minutes.

If your microwave oven has a 'defrost' setting, use it for thawing all foods. It is necessary only to use the microwave power in short bursts for thawing food, and on the 'defrost' setting the oven is automatically switched on and off for a preset period of time. If your oven does not have a 'defrost' setting, thaw food at

30% (low) and turn the oven on and off at regular intervals.

As with conventional cooking, some foods, such as vegetables, may be cooked straight from frozen on 100% (high). Fish can be cooked when only partially thawed. Large, dense pieces of meat and all poultry, however, must be completely thawed before cooking. When thawing, remove food from the microwave oven while still cool to the touch and icy in the center. Thawing will be completed during standing time.

Meat, fish, poultry, casseroles and vegetables should always be covered for thawing. Rolls and bread should be wrapped in absorbent paper towels, but cakes and pies should be thawed uncovered as the melting ice crystals may make them soggy.

If food is left in the microwave oven to thaw for too long, it will begin to cook, so watch the time carefully. If necessary, some thin parts of unevenly shaped food may be shielded with foil (see page 11) to prevent this.

Reheating
All types of food may be reheated in a microwave oven. Portions of food may be arranged on a plate and reheated for latecomers. Place the thickest foods around the edge of the plate and those that will heat through most quickly, such as small vegetables, in the center. Cover with a non-metallic lid or another plate, or with plastic wrap, pierced to allow steam to escape.

When the food is heated right through, the center of the base of the container will feel hot to the touch where heat has been generated from the food.

Always cover food when reheating in a microwave oven, and foods like rice, vegetables or casseroles should be stirred from time to time to distribute the heat evenly and quickly.

B·A·S·I·C K·N·O·W-H·O·W

 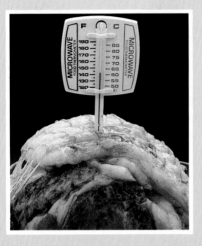

A microwave food thermometer allows for precise timing, especially when cooking meat. The thermometer should be inserted and left during cooking and standing. The meat should be removed from

the oven when the thermometer registers a certain temperature. During the specified standing time the internal temperature of the meat will rise so that eventually the meat will be completely cooked.

Testing whether food is cooked
When cooking in a conventional oven, it is usually possible to tell that food is cooked by its appearance. In a microwave oven this is a less reliable test as it is necessary to remove food from the oven before it is completely cooked.

As cooking times are so short, it is wise to check food regularly during cooking. It is always better to undercook than to overcook. If food remains in the microwave oven for too long, the outside surfaces of the food will toughen and dry.

As with conventional ovens, microwave ovens vary slightly so you may need to experiment a little before you can decide with confidence whether or not food is ready to come out of the oven. You should not test to see if food is cooked until after the standing time, then if not completely

cooked, you can return the food to the oven for another minute.
Meat should feel tender when tested with a skewer, and cheaper cuts should be easy to shred with a fork. When cooking roasts you can get a very accurate reading with a microwave thermometer or probe, if your oven has one. Follow your oven manufacturer's directions carefully when using either. A conventional thermometer may also be used but only *outside* the oven, during standing time, *never inside* during cooking.
Poultry and game are cooked if the juices run clear when the thickest part of the thigh is pierced with a skewer, and when drumsticks will move freely in their sockets.
Vegetables need very little cooking and you may need to experiment as tastes differ. Test with a fork until done to your liking.
Rice and pasta will both seem

hard and uncooked when you take them out of the oven, but by the end of the standing time they will be cooked to perfection – just tender when pressed but retaining some 'bite'.

Eggs cook extremely quickly in a microwave oven so they need careful watching. If overcooked they become very tough. Remove shells and prick the yolks of whole eggs to prevent them from bursting. Eggs should be removed from the oven when the whites are still translucent as the yolks cook more quickly than the whites, which will complete cooking after removal from the oven. Scrambled eggs should be taken out of the oven when still rather runny, and egg-based custards should still be soft in the center when removed, but a knife inserted halfway between the outside edge and the center should come out clean.

Fish and shellfish also need to be watched carefully as it is easy to overcook the thin parts. They are ready to be removed from the oven when the thinner parts flake easily with a fork and the thicker parts are still slightly translucent. They will complete cooking during standing time.

Cakes and sponge puddings will still look uncooked and damp on top when they are ready to be removed from the oven, but on standing these damp patches will disappear. It is important to take them out of the oven at this stage as there's no saving an overcooked cake. On removal, it should be possible to ease the side of the cake away from the dish, and a wooden cocktail pick inserted in the center (though not through a damp spot) should come out clean.

Pastry will have a dry and puffy appearance when it is cooked, perhaps with a few brown spots called 'hot spots'. These are caused when the microwaves are attracted to certain spots because of an uneven distribution of fat in the dough.

USING THE RECIPES IN THIS BOOK

With practice, you will soon become confident enough to cook whole meals in the microwave oven without once turning on your conventional oven.

To help with planning meals, you will find the cooking time, standing time and oven setting given at the beginning of each recipe in the following chapters. To make things as clear as possible, the power settings are given in the recipes in percentages – 100%, 70%, 50% and 30%. We classify these percentages as 'high', 'medium high', 'medium' and 'low'. Check your handbook as your oven may define low differently or may have settings labelled 'roast', 'simmer', 'reheat', etc. – your oven handbook will tell you exactly what percentage of full power each setting represents.

The cooking time given at the beginning of each recipe is the minimum total time for cooking in a 700-watt oven. It is intended as an approximate guide and does not include preparation time. If you are using a 600-watt oven you will need to add 20 seconds per minute to the times given in the recipes. For a 500-watt oven you may need to add as much as 40 seconds per minute. Do not test food until after the standing time.

As ovens vary and timing can be affected by so many factors (see page 13) you may need to experiment with cooking times a little at first. The best policy is to cook food for a little less time than you think is needed, then to cook for a minute or two more if necessary. Remember – in a microwave oven it is better to undercook than to overcook first.

B·A·S·I·C K·N·O·W-H·O·W

If strong-flavored foods leave lingering smells, place a bowl containing 4 parts water and 1 part lemon juice in the oven and microwave at 100% (high) for 7-8 minutes.

S·O·U·P·S

Lima Bean & Celery Soup

LIMA BEAN & CELERY SOUP

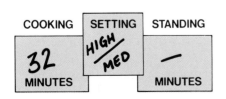

COOKING	SETTING	STANDING
32 MINUTES	HIGH/MED	— MINUTES

2 packages (10 oz size) frozen lima beans
4 celery stalks, chopped
5 cups boiling chicken stock
1 teaspoon chopped fresh thyme or ½ teaspoon dried thyme
salt and pepper
watercress sprigs, for garnish

Serves 4-6

1 Put the lima beans, celery, stock, thyme and salt and pepper to taste into a 2 quart casserole. Cover and microwave at 100% (high) for 20 minutes. Skim off any foam with a slotted spoon, re-cover and microwave at 50% (medium) for 10 minutes, or until the vegetables are very soft and thoroughly cooked.

2 Let the soup cool a little, then press it through a strainer, or purée in a blender or food processor. Return the soup to the rinsed-out casserole, taste and adjust seasoning if necessary.

3 Cover casserole and microwave at 100% (high) for 2 minutes, to reheat, then pour into 4-6 warmed individual soup bowls. Garnish with a few small sprigs of watercress and serve.

CORN & TUNA CHOWDER

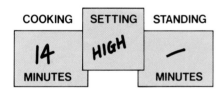

COOKING	SETTING	STANDING
14 MINUTES	HIGH	— MINUTES

2 tablespoons margarine
1 large onion, minced
¼ cup all-purpose flour
2 teaspoons paprika
pinch of cayenne
3¾ cups milk
¼ teaspoon salt
grated rind of ½ lemon
1 package (10 oz) frozen whole kernel corn
1 can (6½ oz) tuna, drained and flaked
For the garnish:
4 tablespoons chopped fresh parsley
½ cup shredded Cheddar cheese

Serves 4-6

1 Place the margarine in a 3 quart bowl, add the onion and microwave for 3 minutes at 100% (high), stirring after 2 minutes.

2 Stir in the flour, paprika and cayenne. Gradually add 1¼ cups of the milk, stirring thoroughly to mix. Microwave at 100% (high) for 3-4 minutes, or until boiling, stirring 2-3 times.

3 Stir in the remaining milk and cook for 3-4 minutes at 100% (high). Add the salt and lemon.

Beefy Soup

4 Add the corn, cover with pierced plastic wrap and microwave at 100% (high) for 3-4 minutes.

5 Add the tuna, re-cover and microwave at 100% (high) for a further 2 minutes, until heated through.

6 Taste and adjust seasoning, then pour into warmed individual serving bowls. Sprinkle with chopped parsley and shredded cheese and serve.

BEEFY SOUP

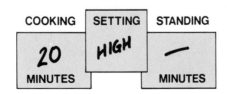

COOKING	SETTING	STANDING
20 MINUTES	HIGH	— MINUTES

3 tablespoons margarine or butter
2 onions, minced
1 potato, diced (½ inch pieces)
1 large green pepper, seeded and cut in chunks
2 teaspoons paprika
2 tablespoons tomato paste
1 lb lean ground beef
4 cups hot beef stock

¾ of a 10 oz package frozen whole kernel corn
salt and pepper
For the garnish:
⅔ cup sour cream
1 tablespoon chopped chives

Serves 4-6

1 Place the margarine in a 2 quart casserole with the onions and potato and microwave at 100% (high) for 4 minutes. Add the green pepper and microwave at 100% (high) for 3 minutes, stirring 2-3 times.

2 Sprinkle the paprika into the casserole, add the tomato paste and lean ground beef and stir to remove any lumps. Microwave at 100% (high) for 5 minutes, stirring 2-3 times.

3 Add the beef stock, cover and microwave at 100% (high) for 5 minutes. Stir in the corn, add salt and pepper to taste, re-cover and microwave at 100% (high) for 3-4 minutes to heat through.

4 Pour into warmed soup bowls and top each with a swirl of sour cream. Sprinkle with chopped chives and serve immediately.

RED PEPPER SOUP

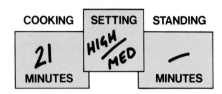

COOKING	SETTING	STANDING
21 MINUTES	HIGH/MED	— MINUTES

1/4 cup oil
3 onions, chopped
2 large sweet red peppers,
    seeded and chopped
3 tablespoons all-purpose flour
3 cups chicken stock
2 tablespoons tomato paste
1 tablespoon chopped chives
salt and pepper
For the garnish:
4 bacon slices, chopped
1 tablespoon chopped chives

Serves 4

1 Place the oil in a 2 quart casserole. Add the onions and peppers, cover and microwave at 100% (high) for 5 minutes, stirring twice.
2 Stir in the flour, then gradually stir in the stock and tomato paste. Microwave at 100% (high) for 3 minutes, or until thick, stirring 2-3 times.
3 Add the chives and salt and pepper to taste; cover and microwave at 50% (medium) for 10 minutes. Let the soup cool slightly, then purée in a blender or food processor.
4 For the garnish, place the bacon on a plate, cover with a sheet of paper towels and then microwave at 100% (high) for 1-2 minutes, or until cooked, stirring twice.
5 Return the soup to the rinsed out casserole and microwave at 100% (high) for 2 minutes. Ladle into bowls, sprinkle with bacon and chives and serve.

M·I·C·R·O·T·I·P

For a croûton garnish, heat 2 tablespoons butter at 100% (high) for 1 minute. Add 1 cup bread cubes, stir and cook at 100% (high) for 2 minutes, stirring once. Sprinkle over bowls of soup.

MUSSEL SOUP

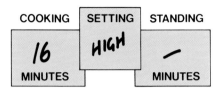

COOKING	SETTING	STANDING
16 MINUTES	HIGH	— MINUTES

1 1/4 cups dry white wine
4 shallots, minced
1 bay leaf
a few sprigs of parsley
2 tablespoons olive oil
salt and white pepper
2 quarts mussels, cleaned
2 tablespoons margarine or butter
1 fennel bulb, chopped
3 celery stalks, sliced
1/2 sweet red pepper, seeded
    and sliced
4 tomatoes, seeded and chopped
2 cups sliced button mushrooms
2/3 cup heavy cream
1 tablespoon dry vermouth

Serves 4

1 Pour the wine into a large bowl. Add half the shallots, the bay leaf, parsley sprigs and 1 tablespoon olive oil. Season with salt.
2 Cover with pierced plastic wrap and microwave at 100% (high) for 4 minutes, until boiling.
3 Add the mussels, re-cover and microwave at 100% (high) for 3-4 minutes until the mussels open.
4 Lift out the mussels with a slotted spoon and discard any that are closed. Remove top shells. Keep the mussels warm. Strain and reserve the liquid.
5 Place the remaining oil and shallots in a large bowl with the margarine, fennel, celery and sweet red pepper. Microwave at 100% (high) for 4 minutes. Add the tomatoes and mushrooms, stir and microwave at 100% (high) for 2 minutes.
6 Add the cream, the reserved cooking liquid and the vermouth. Add salt and white pepper to taste and microwave at 100% (high) for 3 minutes. Stir in the mussels and serve.

Red Pepper Soup

ASPARAGUS SOUP WITH GARLIC ROLLS

COOKING	SETTING	STANDING
17½ MINUTES	HIGH	— MINUTES

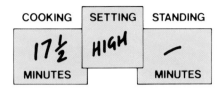

1 lb fresh asparagus, trimmed
  of woody stems
5 scallions
1 onion, chopped
¼ cup margarine or butter
2½ cups hot vegetable stock
6 tablespoons all-purpose flour
1¼ cups milk
3 tablespoons heavy cream
2 wholewheat bread rolls
1 package (2¾ oz) semisoft
  cheese with garlic
  and herbs
1 tablespoon chopped fresh
  mixed herbs or parsley

Serves 4

1 Cut the asparagus stems in short lengths and set the tips aside. Thinly slice the scallions, keeping the green and white parts separate. Separate the white parts into rings and reserve.
2 Place the green onion stems in a 2 quart casserole, add the asparagus stems, onion, butter and half the stock. Cover tightly with lid or pierced plastic wrap and microwave at 100% (high) for 9 minutes. Stir after 5 minutes.
3 Gradually mix the remaining stock with the flour, stirring constantly. Stir in a little of the hot soup, then pour the mixture back into the casserole. Microwave at 100% (high) for 2-3 minutes, or until thick.
4 Let soup cool slightly, then work in a blender or food processor. Stir in the milk. Put the reserved asparagus tips in a small bowl with ¼ cup water. Cover with pierced plastic wrap and

Asparagus Soup with Garlic Rolls

microwave at 100% (high) for 4 minutes. Add the scallions recover and microwave at 100% (high) for 1 minute, then drain.
5 Reheat the soup, covered with lid, at 100% (high) for 1-2 minutes, then stir in the cream. Meanwhile cut the rolls in half and spread with the cheese. Place around the edge of a plate lined with paper towels. Microwave at 100% (high) for 30-60 seconds, to melt cheese.
6 Serve the soup in bowls garnished with the asparagus tips and scallion rings. Serve rolls sprinkled with chopped herbs.

M·I·C·R·O·T·I·P

If fresh asparagus is not available, use 1 lb frozen whole asparagus spears. Follow step 2, microwaving the frozen asparagus for 12-14 minutes instead of 9 minutes, and rearranging the asparagus halfway through. After cooking, cut the asparagus stems into short lengths and set the tips aside for the garnish.

MIXED VEGETABLE SOUP

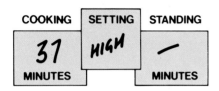

COOKING	SETTING	STANDING
37 MINUTES	HIGH	— MINUTES

2 tablespoons butter or
 margarine
1 leek, thinly sliced
1 onion, thinly sliced
2 carrots, cut in thick slices
2 potatoes, diced
2 celery stalks, diced
4 cans (8 oz each) chicken
 consommé, made up to 5 cups
 with water
1 tablespoon minced fresh
 parsley
½ teaspoon dried marjoram
½ teaspoon salt
1 tomato, peeled and chopped
½ cup frozen wax beans
½ cup frozen whole kernel corn
½ of a 10 oz package frozen
 cauliflower flowerets
½ cup shredded Cheddar
 cheese, for garnish

Serves 4

1 Combine the butter, leek and onion in a 3 quart casserole. Cover and microwave at 100% (high) for 1-1½ minutes or until the vegetables are soft.
2 Add the carrots, potatoes and celery. Re-cover and microwave at 100% (high) for 5 minutes, stirring once.
3 Add the consommé, herbs and salt. Cover and microwave at 100% (high) for 23-25 minutes, until the vegetables are almost tender, stirring once.
4 Stir in the chopped tomato, frozen beans, corn and cauliflower. Cover and microwave at 100% (high) for 8-10 minutes until the vegetables are tender and cooked through.
5 Divide among 4 soup bowls and serve with the cheese.

Lentil & Ham Soup

MUSHROOM SOUP

COOKING	SETTING	STANDING
12 MINUTES	HIGH	1 MINUTES

1 large onion, minced
3 tablespoons butter
3 cups finely sliced mushrooms
½ teaspoon ground coriander
1 tablespoon all-purpose flour
4 cups chicken stock
⅔ cup dry white wine
⅔ cup light cream
salt and pepper
chopped fresh parsley, for garnish

Serves 6-8

1 Place the onion and butter in a large bowl and cover with pierced plastic wrap. Microwave at 100% (high) for 3-4 minutes.
2 Stir in the mushrooms and co-riander. Re-cover and mic-rowave at 100% (high) for 2 minutes.
3 Stir in the flour and gradually add the stock, then microwave, uncovered, at 100% (high) for 5 minutes. Stir in the wine and microwave at 100% (high) for 2 minutes. Purée in a blender.
4 Stir in half the cream, season to taste and stand for 1 minute.
5 Pour into bowls, swirl on the remaining cream and sprinkle with chopped parsley.

LENTIL & HAM SOUP

COOKING	SETTING	STANDING
16 MINUTES	HIGH	— MINUTES

½ cup split red lentils
1 large onion, chopped
2 carrots, chopped

Mushroom Soup

2 celery stalks, chopped
4 cups boiling water
2-3 chicken bouillon cubes
¼ teaspoon dried mixed herbs
1 cup diced cooked ham, to
  finish
salt and pepper

Serves 4

1 Combine the lentils, onion, carrots, celery, water, crumbled bouillon cubes and herbs in a large bowl. Cover with pierced plastic wrap.
2 Microwave at 100% (high) for 8-10 minutes, until water boils, stirring twice, then for a further 8-9 minutes or until lentils are tender, stirring twice.
3 In a blender or food processor, purée the mixture until smooth. Stir in ham, season and serve.

MINESTRONE SOUP

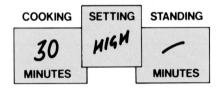

COOKING	SETTING	STANDING
30 MINUTES	*HIGH*	⁃ MINUTES

2 celery stalks, thinly sliced
2 carrots, thinly sliced
1 cup shredded cabbage
2 garlic cloves, crushed
1 large potato, diced
1 can (16 oz) chopped tomatoes
2 zucchini, thinly sliced
1½ cups cut green beans
¼ cup ditalini
4 cups hot water
2 beef bouillon cubes, crumbled
1 teaspoon dried oregano

Serves 6

1 In a 3 quart casserole, mix all ingredients, then cover with pierced plastic wrap.
2 Microwave at 100% (high) for 30-35 minutes or until vegetables are tender. Stir once or twice. Serve immediately.

CORNED BEEF SOUP

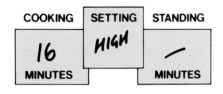

COOKING	SETTING	STANDING
16 MINUTES	HIGH	— MINUTES

2 tablespoons vegetable oil
1 large onion, chopped
1½ cups carrots, in ¼ inch dice
2½ cups potatoes, in ¼ inch dice
3 cups hot beef stock
1 can (about 8 oz) corned beef, diced
salt and pepper
chopped fresh parsley, for garnish
grated Parmesan cheese, for garnish (optional)

Serves 4

1 Place the oil and onion in a 2 quart casserole and microwave at 100% (high) for 2 minutes. Add the carrots and potatoes, cover with the lid or pierced plastic wrap and microwave at 100% (high) for 6 minutes; stir once.
2 Pour in the stock, re-cover and microwave at 100% (high) for 6 minutes, or until the carrots and potatoes are just tender.
3 Add the corned beef and season to taste with salt and pepper. Re-cover and microwave at 100% (high) for 2 minutes. Serve sprinkled with parsley. Pass the cheese separately if wished.

CORN CHOWDER

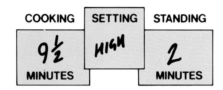

COOKING	SETTING	STANDING
9½ MINUTES	HIGH	2 MINUTES

3 Canadian bacon slices, chopped
1 small onion, minced
2½ cups milk
2 tablespoons all-purpose flour
1 can (8 oz) cream-style corn
1 can (8 oz) whole kernel corn, drained
1 tablespoon chopped fresh parsley
1 small egg, beaten
salt and pepper
½ teaspoon paprika (optional)
2-3 tablespoons sour cream

Serves 6

1 Place the bacon and onion in a large casserole. Microwave at 100% (high) for 2-3 minutes, or until the bacon is colored and onion tender, stirring once.
2 Gradually blend 1¼ cups milk with the flour. Stir into the onion mixture and microwave at 100% (high) for 1½ minutes until thick and bubbling, stirring once.
3 Beat in the remaining milk, then stir in the corn, parsley, egg and seasoning. Microwave at 100% (high) for 6-7 minutes until

Corn Chowder

smooth and hot, stirring several times. Let stand for 2-3 minutes.
4 Serve hot or chilled. Sprinkle with paprika, if liked. Swirl in the sour cream to serve.

CREAMY TOMATO SOUP

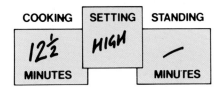

COOKING	SETTING	STANDING
12½ MINUTES	HIGH	— MINUTES

1 lb ripe tomatoes, chopped
½ onion, minced
2 teaspoons sugar
1 bay leaf
1 tablespoon butter or
    margarine
1 tablespoon all-purpose flour
1¼ cups milk
2 cups boiling water
3 tablespoons tomato paste
2 vegetable or chicken bouillon
    cubes
salt and pepper
¼ cup light cream

Serves 4

1 Combine the tomatoes, onion, sugar and bay leaf in a small bowl. Cover with pierced plastic wrap and microwave at 100% (high) for 5-8 minutes, stirring once. Push through a strainer. Set pulp aside.
2 Microwave the butter in a covered bowl at 100% (high) for 30-45 seconds. Blend in the flour and milk. Microwave at 100% (high) for 4-5 minutes, stirring once or twice. Mix in the tomato pulp.
3 Pour the boiling water onto the tomato paste and the bouillon cubes. Stir then blend into the soup.
4 Season with salt and pepper. Microwave at 100% (high) for 3 minutes, stirring once; do not let boil. Spoon into dishes and swirl cream on top.

Creamy Tomato Soup

VICHYSSOISE

COOKING	SETTING	STANDING
28 MINUTES	HIGH	— MINUTES

¼ cup butter
1½ cups thinly sliced leeks,
    white parts only, washed
1 large onion, thinly sliced
1 medium-size potato, peeled
    and thinly sliced
4 cups hot chicken stock
salt and pepper
⅔ cups heavy cream, to
    serve
chopped chives, for garnish

Serves 4

1 Put the butter in a very large heatproof bowl or casserole. Microwave at 100% (high) for 3 minutes, stirring frequently, until the butter has melted.
2 Add the leek and onion slices to the butter and mix well. Microwave, uncovered, at 100% (high) for 5 minutes, stirring frequently, until the leeks and onion are soft.
3 Add the potato slices and chicken stock, mix well, then cover with pierced plastic wrap. Microwave at 100% (high) for 20 minutes, or until the potatoes are soft, stirring every 5 minutes.
4 Let the soup cool a little then purée in an electric blender or food processor until smooth. Season the soup well with salt and pepper, then return to a bowl and chill for 3-4 hours.
5 Stir the cream into the chilled soup before serving in chilled bowls garnished with chopped chives.

A·P·P·ET·I·Z·E·R·S

Tortellini with Tomato Sauce

TORTELLINI WITH TOMATO SAUCE

COOKING	SETTING	STANDING
11 MINUTES	HIGH	4 MINUTES

1 lb fresh tortellini
1 teaspoon salt
1 tablespoon vegetable oil
4 slices processed cheese
For the sauce:
1 can (16 oz) peeled tomatoes
1 onion, chopped
few sprigs parsley
3 tablespoons margarine
⅓ cup all-purpose flour

1 tablespoon tomato paste
½ teaspoon light brown
   sugar
salt and pepper

Serves 4

1 To make the sauce, place the tomatoes, chopped onion and the parsley sprigs in a blender or food processor and purée.

2 Place the margarine in a 1 quart bowl and microwave at 100% (high) for 30 seconds to melt. Stir in the flour. Gradually stir in the puréed mixture, then add the tomato paste and sugar. Stir in salt and pepper to taste. Microwave at 100% (high) for 2-3 minutes, until thick, stirring 2-3 times.

3 Place the tortellini in a large bowl with 5 cups boiling water, salt and oil. Cover with pierced plastic wrap and microwave at 100% (high) for 8 minutes. Let stand for 4 minutes, then drain and divide the tortellini among 4 individual dishes.

4 Pour the tomato sauce over the top. Place a cheese slice on top of each portion. If wished, cut a cheese animal, using cookie cutters. Place the dishes in the microwave oven and microwave at 100% (high) for 30-45 seconds, or until the cheese has melted. Serve at once.

Ham & Orange Fricassée

HAM & ORANGE FRICASSEE

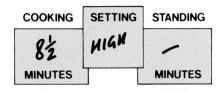

COOKING	SETTING	STANDING
8½	HIGH	—
MINUTES		MINUTES

2 ready-to-eat ham center slices
1 package (10 oz) frozen peas
4 servings instant mashed
  potatoes, made up according
  to package directions
1 teaspoon chopped fresh
  parsley, for garnish
For the sauce:
2 tablespoons margarine or
  butter
¼ cup all-purpose flour
1¼ cups milk
finely grated rind and juice of 1
  small orange
salt and pepper

Serves 4

1 Cut the ham in ¾ inch cubes.
2 To make the sauce, place the margarine in a 2 quart casserole dish and microwave at 100% (high) for 30 seconds, or until melted. Stir in the flour.
3 Gradually add the milk, stirring continuously. Microwave at 100% (high) for 3-4 minutes, or until the sauce is thick, stirring 2-3 times.
4 Add the orange rind, juice and salt and pepper to taste. Stir well, then add the ham and peas. Cover dish with lid or pierced plastic wrap and microwave at 100% (high) for 4 minutes, to heat through.
5 Cover mashed potatoes with pierced plastic wrap, and microwave at 100% (high) for 1-2 minutes, to reheat.
6 To serve, pipe or spoon the potato around the edge of a large serving dish or 4 individual plates. Arrange the fricassée inside the potato ring. Garnish with chopped parsley and serve at once while piping hot.

HAM & CHEESE MUNCHIES

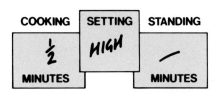

COOKING	SETTING	STANDING
½	HIGH	—
MINUTES		MINUTES

½ cup shredded Monterey Jack
3 tablespoons mayonnaise
2 teaspoons chopped parsley
2 scallions, finely chopped
6 bacon slices, cooked and
  crumbled
12 toast rounds

Makes 12

1 Mix the cheese, mayonnaise, parsley and scallions in a bowl and stir in the bacon.
2 Spread the mixture on the toast and arrange on a paper towel on a plate. Microwave at 100% (high) for 30-45 seconds, rotating the plate a half turn during the cooking. Serve the munchies hot.

CHICKEN LIVER PATE

COOKING	SETTING	STANDING
9 MINUTES	HIGH	— MINUTES

2 tablespoons butter
6 bacon slices, chopped
1 lb frozen chicken livers,
    thawed
1 clove garlic, crushed
1 tablespoon sherry
1 large sprig parsley
1 large sprig fresh thyme or 1
    teaspoon dried thyme
salt and pepper
¼ cup clarified butter
pistachio nuts, for garnish
    (optional)
Accompaniments:
toast triangles, white or
    wholewheat

Serves 4-6

1 Place the butter in a 2 quart casserole. Add the bacon and microwave at 100% (high) for 3-4 minutes, or until the bacon is cooked, stirring 2-3 times.
2 Add the chicken livers and garlic to the casserole and microwave at 100% (high) for 5-6 minutes, stirring 2-3 times.
3 Let cool slightly, then place the chicken livers, and any liquid, in a blender or food processor. Add the sherry, parsley and thyme and purée until thoroughly blended and smooth.
4 Season to taste with salt and pepper. Turn the pâté into a small, deep oval-shaped terrine or 4-6 custard cups and smooth over the top.
5 Microwave the clarified butter at 100% (high) for 45-60 seconds and pour in a thin layer over the pâté. Garnish with pistachio nuts, if using, and refrigerate for at least 1 hour, and up to 1 week, before serving with white or wholewheat toast triangles.

SUNFLOWER SEED PEPPERS

COOKING	SETTING	STANDING
14 MINUTES	HIGH	— MINUTES

2 tablespoons sunflower oil
1 large onion, chopped
1 sweet red pepper, seeded and
    cut into ½ inch squares
1 lb tomatoes, peeled and
    chopped
1 cup quartered button
    mushrooms
¼ cup sunflower seeds,
    toasted
½ teaspoon dried thyme
¼ teaspoon paprika
salt and pepper
4 ripe olives, pitted and
    halved
2 green peppers, seeded and
    halved lengthwise
⅓ cup shredded Edam cheese

Serves 4

1 Place the oil in a 2 quart casserole, add the onion and microwave at 100% (high) for 2 minutes. Add the sweet red pepper, microwave at 100% (high) for 2 minutes, then stir.
2 Add the tomatoes, mushrooms, sunflower seeds, thyme, paprika, salt and pepper, stir, then microwave at 100% (high) for 6 minutes, stirring 2-3 times. Stir in the olives.
3 Place the pepper halves in a large bowl, cover with lightly salted boiling water, cover with pierced plastic wrap and microwave at 100% (high) for 3 minutes. Drain thoroughly.
4 Put the pepper halves in a serving dish and season inside with salt and pepper. Pile in the filling. Sprinkle with cheese and microwave at 100% (high) for 1-2 minutes until the cheese has melted. Serve at once.

Sunflower Seed Peppers

STUFFED ONIONS

COOKING	SETTING	STANDING
24 MINUTES	HIGH	9 MINUTES

4 large Bermuda onions, peeled
chopped fresh parsley, for
*   garnish*
For the sauce:
1 clove garlic, crushed
2 tablespoons margarine or
*   butter*
1 can (16 oz) chopped tomatoes
2 tablespoons tomato paste
salt and pepper
For the stuffing:
½ lb liver pâté
2 tablespoons chopped fresh
*   parsley*
Accompaniments:
3 cups small pasta shapes
1 tablespoon oil

Serves 4

1 Cut a slice from the top of each onion. Using a teaspoon, scoop out the center to leave a shell about ¼ inch thick.
2 To make the sauce, finely chop the scooped-out onion flesh and put it in a small bowl. Add the garlic and margarine, cover with pierced plastic wrap and microwave at 100% (high) for 3 minutes. Stir in tomatoes, tomato paste and season to taste. Re-cover and microwave at 100% (high) for 4 minutes, or until bubbling.
3 Mix the pâté and parsley together and spoon into the onion shells. Arrange the stuffed onions in a ring in a shallow dish and pour the tomato sauce around them. Cover with pierced plastic wrap and microwave at 100% (high) for 12-14 minutes, or until the onions are soft, turning the dish twice during cooking. Let stand, covered, for 7 minutes.
4 Meanwhile put the pasta in a large bowl and add the oil and 4 cups boiling water. Cover with

Stuffed Onions

pierced plastic wrap and microwave at 100% (high) for 5 minutes, until the pasta is just tender. Let stand for 2 minutes, drain and serve with the onions, garnished with chopped parsley.

CHEESY FRANKS

COOKING	SETTING	STANDING
2 MINUTES	HIGH	— MINUTES

6 frankfurters or hot dogs,
*   slit along one edge*
6 frankfurter rolls, slit

2 slices processed cheese, each
*   cut in 3 strips*

Makes 6

1 Place the frankfurters in the slit bread rolls. Place in a single layer on a plate lined with paper towels.
2 Microwave at 100% (high) for 1 minute to heat.
3 Rearrange the rolls on the plate and place a strip of cheese in each sausage slit. Position with slit uppermost.
4 Microwave at 100% (high) for 45-60 seconds to melt the cheese. Serve hot.

HUMMUS WITH TAHINI

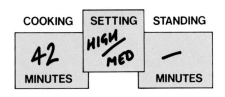

COOKING	SETTING	STANDING
42 MINUTES	HIGH/MED	— MINUTES

½ cup dried chick-peas
¼ cup olive oil
1 large clove garlic, crushed
¼ cup lemon juice
¼ cup tahini paste
salt and pepper
¼ teaspoon paprika
few sprigs of parsley, for
  garnish
Accompaniments:
lemon wedges
pita bread

Serves 4

1 Put the chick-peas into a deep bowl, cover with plenty of cold water and let soak for several hours, or overnight.
2 Drain and rinse the chick-peas, put them in a 2 quart bowl and cover with 3¾ cups cold water. Cover with pierced plastic wrap and microwave at 100% (high) for 12 minutes, or until boiling. Reduce to 50% (medium) for 30 minutes, or until the chick-peas have softened.
3 Drain, reserving the liquid, and let cool.
4 Reserve 12 chick-peas for garnish and put the remainder in an electric blender with half the oil, the garlic, lemon juice, tahini paste and salt and pepper to taste. Blend to a smooth purée, adding a little of the reserved liquid if necessary to give a consistency like thick mayonnaise.

Transfer the hummus to a bowl and refrigerate for a minimum of 1 hour.
5 To serve, spoon the hummus into a shallow dish or 4 individual dishes. Put the paprika in a small bowl and gradually stir in the remaining olive oil to make a smooth paste. Drizzle this over the top of the hummus and garnish with the whole chick-peas and parsley sprigs. Serve chilled with lemon wedges and pita bread.

HAM KABOBS WITH PEANUT DIP

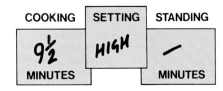

COOKING	SETTING	STANDING
9½ MINUTES	HIGH	— MINUTES

1 lb lean smoked ham shoulder
  butt, trimmed and cut
  in ¾-1 inch cubes
3 tablespoons crunchy peanut
  butter
⅓ cup shredded coconut
⅔ cup water
salt and pepper
coriander leaves,
  for garnish
For the marinade:
2 tablespoons vegetable oil
2 teaspoons curry paste
2 teaspoons lemon juice
½ teaspoon ground
  coriander
¼ teaspoon ground
  turmeric

Serves 4

1 To make the marinade, blend all the ingredients together in a 2 quart casserole.
2 Add the ham cubes and coat thoroughly in the marinade. Cover and leave to marinate for 30 minutes.
3 Remove the ham cubes from the marinade with a slotted spoon. Reserve the marinade.

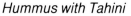
Hummus with Tahini

Ham Kabobs with Peanut Dip

Thread the ham chunks onto 12 wooden kabob sticks.

4 Place the kabobs in a single layer on a large plate. Microwave at 100% (high) for 8 minutes, turning the kabobs, and giving the plate a half turn after 5 minutes.

5 Add the peanut butter, coconut and water to the reserved marinade and season with salt and pepper. Microwave at 100% (high) for 1½-2 minutes, stirring after 1 minute and again at the end of the time.

6 Arrange the kabobs on a warmed serving platter and garnish with coriander. Take 2 tablespoons of juices from the plate on which the kabobs were cooked and stir into the peanut dip. Pour the dip into a warmed bowl and serve at once, surrounded by the kabobs.

CHILIED EGGS

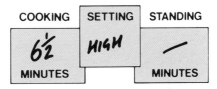

COOKING	SETTING	STANDING
6½ MINUTES	HIGH	— MINUTES

1 onion, minced
¼ inch piece fresh gingerroot, pared and finely chopped
3 tablespoons margarine or butter
1 green chili, seeded and finely chopped
½ teaspoon turmeric
2 tablespoons chopped fresh coriander or parsley
½ teaspoon salt
8 eggs, lightly beaten
tomato wedges, for garnish

Serves 4

1 Place the onion, ginger and margarine in a 2 quart casserole and microwave at 100% (high) for 2 minutes. Add the chili, turmeric, most of the coriander or parsley and the salt.

2 Microwave at 100% (high) for 1 minute. Pour in the eggs, and microwave at 100% (high) for 3½-4 minutes, stirring 3-4 times, until they are softly scrambled.

3 Serve garnished with remaining herbs and tomato wedges.

M·I·C·R·O·T·I·P

Although scrambled eggs will not look cooked on removal from the oven, they will be done to perfection by the time they are garnished and served.

DEVILED CORN TOASTS

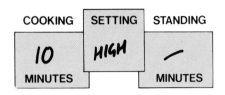

COOKING	SETTING	STANDING
10 MINUTES	HIGH	— MINUTES

8 bacon slices
1/4 cup butter
1 bunch scallions, chopped
1/4 cup light cream
1 cup shredded Cheddar cheese
1 package (10 oz) frozen whole kernel corn, thawed
2 tablespoons Worcestershire sauce
1 teaspoon Dijon mustard
salt and pepper

2 eggs, beaten
4 slices hot toast

Serves 4

1 Place the bacon on a microwave rack or plate lined with paper towels. Cover with a sheet of paper towels. Microwave at 100% (high) for 5-6 minutes. Rearrange after 3 minutes. Drain on papers towels and cover the bacon slices to keep them warm.
2 Place half the butter in a 1 quart bowl, add the scallions and microwave at 100% (high) for 2 minutes. Stir in the cream, cheese, corn, Worcestershire sauce, mustard and seasoning.
3 Add the beaten eggs and microwave at 100% (high) for 3-4 minutes, or until thick, stirring 2-3 times.
4 Spread the remaining butter over the toast and then divide the corn mixture among the slices. Top each with 2 bacon slices and serve at once.

HERBY SPAGHETTI

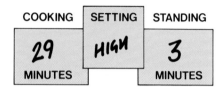

COOKING	SETTING	STANDING
29 MINUTES	HIGH	3 MINUTES

1 lb spaghetti
1 tablespoon olive oil

Deviled Corn Toasts

2 tablespoons butter
½ cup grated Parmesan cheese
2 teaspoons Italian seasoning
salt and pepper
For the sauce:
2 tablespoons olive oil
1 onion, chopped
1 clove garlic, crushed
1 green pepper, seeded and
    chopped
1 cup sliced mushrooms
2 cans (16 oz each) tomatoes
salt and pepper

Serves 4

1 To make the sauce, place the oil in a 2 quart bowl, add the onion, garlic, pepper and mushrooms and microwave at 100% (high) for 4-5 minutes, stirring 2-3 times.
2 Stir in the tomatoes with their juice, breaking them up with a spoon. Add salt and pepper to taste. Microwave at 100% (high) for 15 minutes, stirring 2-3 times. Cover and set aside.
3 Place the spaghetti in a 3 quart bowl with 7½ cups boiling salted water. As the spaghetti softens, push it under the water or break in half if necessary. Add the olive oil.
4 Cover with pierced plastic wrap and microwave at 100% (high) for 8 minutes.
5 Let stand for 3 minutes, then drain. Add the butter, half the Parmesan, the Italian seasoning and salt and pepper to taste. Toss

Cheese & Chicken Pockets

to coat, and transfer to a warmed serving dish.
6 Microwave the sauce at 100% (high) for 2 minutes, adjust the seasoning, and pour over the spaghetti. Sprinkle with the remaining grated Parmesan and serve at once.

CHEESE & CHICKEN POCKETS

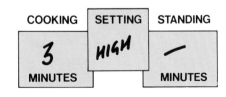

COOKING	SETTING	STANDING
3 MINUTES	**HIGH**	**—** MINUTES

4 pita breads
1 small green pepper, seeded
    and sliced in thin rings
7 oz Gruyère cheese, cut in
    thin strips
2 large firm tomatoes, thinly
    sliced

8 slices cooked chicken
    (around 6 oz)
salt and pepper
3 tablespoons mango chutney

Serves 4

1 Cut each pita bread in half crosswise and ease the pockets open with a knife, taking care not to pierce the sides of the bread.
2 Divide the remaining ingredients into 8 portions, then hold each pita pocket open with one hand and, with the other, layer the ingredients into the pockets in the following order: green pepper, cheese, tomato and chicken. As you complete each layer, sprinkle it with a little salt and pepper, then spread the chicken with chutney.
3 Arrange around the edge of a large plate, with filling toward the outside, and microwave at 100% (high) for 3-4 minutes. Give the plate a half turn after 2 minutes. Serve at once.

TOMATO & EGG BAKES

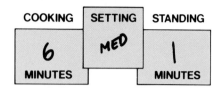

COOKING	SETTING	STANDING
6 MINUTES	MED	1 MINUTES

4 tomatoes, peeled
1 teaspoon chopped fresh basil
   or ½ teaspoon dried basil
salt and pepper
4 large eggs
basil leaves, for garnish
   (optional)

Serves 4

1 Dice the tomatoes and divide among 4 individual ⅔ cup dishes or custard cups.
2 Sprinkle a little basil into each dish, and season to taste with salt and pepper. Mix well.
3 Break 1 egg into each dish on top of the tomato and herb mixture. Prick the yolk of each egg twice with a cocktail pick.
4 Cover each dish or custard cup with pierced plastic wrap, then microwave at 50% (medium) for 6-8 minutes. Rotate each dish every 2 minutes. Each dish may not cook at the same speed, so remove as cooked.
5 Let stand for 1 minute, for whites to finish setting, then serve. Garnish with basil leaves if wished.

DUTCH FONDUE

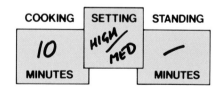

COOKING	SETTING	STANDING
10 MINUTES	HIGH/MED	— MINUTES

2 cups finely chopped
   mushrooms (including stems)
2½ cups hot chicken stock
4 tablespoons cornstarch
⅓ cup milk
2 cups shredded Edam cheese

Tomato & Egg Bakes

1 tablespoon minced fresh
   parsley
1 teaspoon Worcestershire
   sauce
salt and pepper
mushroom slices,
   for garnish
Accompaniments:
1 small French loaf, cut in 1 inch
   cubes
1 lb breakfast mini sausage
   links, cooked and
   thickly sliced
2 cups cauliflower flowerets,
   lightly cooked
2 cups broccoli flowerets,
   lightly cooked

Serves 4-6

1 Place the chopped mushrooms and stock in a 2 quart bowl. Cover with pierced plastic wrap and microwave at 100% (high) for 5 minutes.
2 In a small bowl, mix the cornstarch to a smooth paste with a little of the milk. Stir into the mushroom stock, then add the remaining milk. Re-cover and microwave at 100% (high) for 2 minutes, stirring once.
3 Add the shredded cheese, 2 tablespoons at a time, stirring well, until it has melted. Microwave at 50% (medium) for 3 minutes, stirring occasionally.
4 Stir in the parsley, Worcestershire sauce and salt and pepper. Pour into a fondue pot or 4 individual bowls, garnish with mushroom slices and serve at once.
5 Pass the bread cubes, sausages and vegetables separately, providing forks for dipping them into the fondue.

SAUSAGE & BACON PITAS

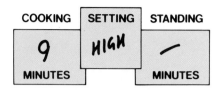

COOKING	SETTING	STANDING
9 MINUTES	HIGH	— MINUTES

1 tablespoon vegetable oil
16 mini pork sausage links
8 bacon slices, each cut in four
2 tablespoons margarine or
butter
1 tablespoon Dijon mustard
¼ teaspoon Worcestershire
sauce
4 small tomatoes, halved
8 pickled onions
4 wholewheat pita breads
4 lettuce leaves

Serves 4

1 Preheat a browning dish at 100% (high) for 5 minutes, or according to manufacturer's directions. Add the oil and sausages and microwave at 100% (high) for 3-4 minutes, turning twice.
2 Place the bacon in a single layer on a plate lined with absorbent kitchen paper towels. Cover with more paper towels and microwave at 100% (high) for 4-5 minutes, rearranging midway through the cooking time.
3 Mix together the margarine, mustard and Worcestershire sauce. Place the tomatoes on a plate and dot with some of the flavored margarine. Microwave at 100% (high) for 1-2 minutes.
4 Slit open the pitas and fill each with an equal amount of sausages, bacon, tomatoes and onions.
5 Place on a large platter, dot remaining flavored margarine over the fillings, and microwave at 100% (high) for 1-1½ minutes, until pita breads are warm and margarine has melted.
6 Place a lettuce leaf in each pita pocket and serve immediately.

BEEFY BEAN TACOS

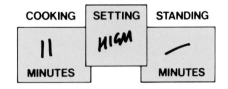

COOKING	SETTING	STANDING
11 MINUTES	HIGH	— MINUTES

1 tablespoon vegetable oil
1 onion, minced
½ lb ground beef
1 can (8 oz) tomatoes, drained
and chopped
2 tablespoons tomato paste
2 teaspoons cornstarch
1 can (8 oz) baked beans
salt and pepper
6 taco shells
For the garnish:
shredded Cheddar cheese
shredded lettuce
2 scallions, chopped

Makes 6

1 Place the oil and onion in a large bowl and microwave at 100% (high) for 2 minutes. Add the beef and microwave at 100% (high) for 4 minutes, stirring at 1 minute intervals to break up the meat.
2 Mix the tomatoes with the tomato paste and cornstarch, then add to the ground beef with the baked beans. Stir. Cover with pierced plastic wrap and microwave at 100% (high) for 4 minutes, or until thick. Add salt and pepper to taste.
3 Place the taco shells upright in an oblong dish, and fill with bean and beef mixture. Microwave at 100% (high) for 1 minute.
4 Garnish with lettuce, cheese and scallions if wished. Serve at once.

M·I·C·R·O·T·I·P

To quickly warm frozen pitas, wrap each in paper towels and microwave at 100% (high) for 20 seconds.

Beefy Bean Tacos

CRAB & CHEESE FLORENTINES

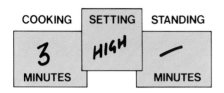

COOKING	SETTING	STANDING
3 MINUTES	*HIGH*	— MINUTES

1½ cups shredded fresh
  spinach
3 tablespoons lemon juice
salt and pepper
6 oz frozen crabmeat, thawed
¾ cup cottage cheese
3 tablespoons plain yogurt
2 teaspoons tomato paste
1 teaspoon Worcestershire
  sauce
2 scallions, minced
1 tablespoon chopped chives
For the garnish (optional):
cayenne
radish roses

Serves 4

1 Put the spinach in a large bowl, add the lemon juice, season well with salt and pepper and toss with two forks, to coat thoroughly.
2 In a 1 quart bowl, mix together the crabmeat, cottage cheese, yogurt, tomato paste, Worcestershire sauce, scallions and chives. Season well and microwave at 100% (high) for 2-3 minutes, stirring 3-4 times, until heated.
3 Microwave the spinach at 100% (high) for 1-1½ minutes, until heated. Stir.
4 Line 4 individual dishes with spinach and top with the crab and cheese mix.
5 To make radish roses, if wished, cut 5 shallow slices around a radish, cutting from the top almost to the base. Place in ice-cold water until the 'petals' open. Arrange on a round of very thin radish slices.
6 Serve the florentines sprinkled with cayenne and garnished with radish roses, if used.

Crab & Cheese Florentines

SOUSED HERRINGS

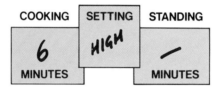

COOKING	SETTING	STANDING
6 MINUTES	*HIGH*	— MINUTES

4 large herring, each about ½ lb
  boned but left in 1 piece
salt and pepper
1 small onion, sliced
⅔ cup white wine vinegar
½ cup water
4 bay leaves
8 whole black peppercorns
1 stick cinnamon, 1 inch long
lemon wedges, for garnish
  (optional)
For the sauce:
2 teaspoons creamed
  horseradish sauce
pinch of dry mustard
⅔ cup heavy cream

Serves 4

1 Season the herring with salt and pepper and roll them up, starting from the head end, with skin on the outside. Secure with wooden cocktail picks, if necessary. Arrange them in a single layer in a dish just large enough to hold them comfortably.
2 Add the onion, vinegar and water and push the bay leaves, peppercorns and cinnamon among the herring. Cover with pierced plastic wrap and microwave at 100% (high) for 6-8 minutes. Give the dish a half turn after 4 minutes. Let cool in the cooking liquid for 8 hours.
3 Drain the herrings, reserving ¼ cup cooking liquid, and place on a serving dish.
4 Put the reserved liquid into a bowl with the horseradish sauce, dry mustard and cream and beat until soft peaks form.
5 Spoon a little sauce over each herring and garnish with lemon wedges, if liked. Serve cold, and pass remaining sauce separately.

SHRIMP PAPRIKA

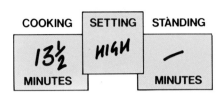

COOKING	SETTING	STANDING
13½ MINUTES	HIGH	— MINUTES

1 can (16 oz) tomatoes
1 large onion, thinly sliced
1 green pepper, seeded and
    sliced
2 tablespoons vegetable oil
1 tablespoon mild paprika
2 cloves garlic, crushed
2 vegetable bouillon cubes
2 teaspoons cornstarch
1 lb shelled jumbo shrimp,
    thawed if frozen,
    deveined
⅔ cup sour cream
salt and pepper
chopped fresh parsley, for
    garnish

Serves 4

1 Drain the tomatoes over a bowl, then roughly chop them. Let the juice stand for 10 minutes, then discard the liquid that rises to the top, leaving behind the pure tomato juice.
2 Put the onion, pepper and oil into a large casserole. Microwave at 100% (high) for 5 minutes, until the vegetables are soft, stirring once during cooking.
3 Stir in the paprika, garlic and crumbled bouillon cubes. Microwave at 100% (high) for 2 minutes.
4 Mix the cornstarch to a paste with a little of the tomato juice; add to remaining juice. Stir into the onion and pepper mixture with the tomatoes. Cover the dish with pierced plastic wrap and microwave at 100% (high) for 3 minutes. Add shrimp and microwave at 100% (high) for a further 2½ minutes, turning the shrimp 2 or 3 times to ensure even cooking.
5 Stir in the sour cream and season well. Microwave at 100%

Seafood Cups

(high) for 1-2 minutes more. Sprinkle with chopped parsley and serve at once.

SEAFOOD CUPS

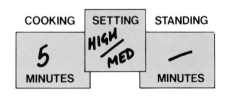

COOKING	SETTING	STANDING
5 MINUTES	HIGH/MED	— MINUTES

2 cups soft white bread crumbs
2 eggs, lightly beaten
1½ cups frozen shelled shrimp,
    thawed
2 tablespoons plain yogurt
¾ cup cottage cheese
2 tablespoons chopped parsley
salt and pepper
tomato slices, for garnish

Serves 4

1 Stir the bread crumbs into the beaten eggs and let stand for 5 minutes so that the crumbs soak up the egg.
2 Reserve a few shrimp for garnish and mix the remainder into the bread crumb mixture, together with the yogurt, cottage cheese and chopped parsley, and stir to ensure that all the ingredients are well blended. Season with salt and pepper.
3 Divide the mixture among 4 greased custard cups. Arrange in a ring in the oven and microwave at 100% (high) for 3 minutes. Give the cups a half turn, reduce power to 50% (medium) and microwave for 2-3 minutes until set.
4 Garnish each cup with slices of tomato and some of the reserved shrimp.

Tangy Fish Sticks

TANGY FISH STICKS

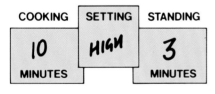

COOKING	SETTING	STANDING
10 MINUTES	HIGH	3 MINUTES

10 breaded fish sticks
4 cups cooked long-grain rice
For the sauce:
2 tablespoons cornstarch
⅔ cup hot chicken stock
1 can (8 oz) pineapple chunks
2 tablespoons soy sauce
pinch of ground ginger
2 teaspoons tomato paste
2 tablespoons light brown sugar
1 tablespoon vinegar
salt and pepper
¼ sweet red pepper, seeded and diced
2 scallions, chopped

Serves 4

1 Make the sauce. In a 2 quart casserole, mix the cornstarch with a little stock, then stir in the remaining stock. Add the pineapple with its juice. Stir in the remaining sauce ingredients.
2 Cover the sauce with pierced plastic wrap and then microwave at 100% (high) for 3-4 minutes, or until the sauce is thick, stirring 2-3 times.
3 Place the fish sticks on a microwave rack and cook, uncovered, at 100% (high) for 4 minutes, rearranging and turning midway through the cooking time. Let stand while you reheat the rice.
4 Place the cooked rice in a bowl, cover with pierced plastic wrap and microwave at 100% (high) for 3-4 minutes until the rice is heated through.
5 Divide the rice among 4 warmed plates. Cut each fish stick in 3 or 4 and place on top. Spoon the sauce over each portion and serve.

SHRIMP WITH PINEAPPLE

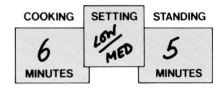

COOKING	SETTING	STANDING
6 MINUTES	LOW/MED	5 MINUTES

1 package (10 oz) frozen shelled shrimp
1 cup Catalina French dressing
1 can (8 oz) pineapple chunks
2 tablespoons tomato paste

Serves 4

1 Spread out shrimp in a single layer in a shallow dish. Cover with pierced plastic wrap. Microwave at 30% (low) for 1-2 minutes. Stir and break up any frozen shrimp. Re-cover and microwave again at 30% (low) for 1-2 minutes.
2 In a 2 quart casserole, mix together the French dressing, pineapple chunks with the juice, tomato paste and the shrimp, cover the casserole with the lid or pierced plastic wrap.
3 Microwave at 50% (medium) for 4-5 minutes, or until hot, stirring every 2 minutes. Let stand for 5 minutes, covered. Serve hot or cold.

SMOKED FISH MOUSSE

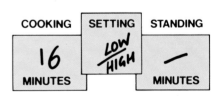

COOKING	SETTING	STANDING
16 MINUTES	LOW/HIGH	— MINUTES

1¼ cups milk
1 small onion
1 small carrot
1 bay leaf
6 black peppercorns
¾ lb smoked haddock
2 tablespoons butter
¼ cup all-purpose flour
pepper

1 envelope unflavored gelatin
⅓ cup cold chicken stock
2 hard-cooked eggs, chopped
1 tablespoon chopped fresh
  parsley
finely grated rind of 1 lemon
1-1½ tablespoons lemon juice
⅔ cup heavy cream whipped
For the garnish:
4 cooked shrimp, in shells
watercress

Serves 4-6

1 Place the milk, onion, carrot, bay leaf and peppercorns in a liquid measure and microwave at 30% (low) for 10 minutes. Place the fish in a dish with 1 tablespoon water, cover with pierced plastic wrap and microwave at 100% (high) for 4 minutes, or until cooked. Skin and flake.

2 Place the butter in a bowl and microwave at 100% (high) for 30-45 seconds to melt. Add the flour, mixing well. Strain the milk and gradually add to the flour mixture, stirring continuously. Microwave at 100% (high) for 1-2 minutes, beating every 30 seconds until the sauce is thick and smooth. Add a little pepper to taste, cover surface with wet waxed paper and let sauce cool.

3 Soak the gelatin in the chicken stock in a small bowl for 2 minutes, then microwave at 100% (high) for 30-45 seconds until gelatin is dissolved. Cool slightly then add to the sauce.

4 Add the flaked fish, eggs, parsley and lemon rind and juice to the sauce and mix well. Fold in the cream, then pour into a 4 cup ring mold and leave to set.

5 Dip the mold briefly into very hot water, then invert mousse on a plate. Garnish with shrimp and watercress and serve with bread rolls or crackers.

Smoked Fish Mousse

M·E·A·T D·I·S·H·E·S

Lime Lamb Roast

LIME LAMB ROAST

COOKING	SETTING	STANDING
47 MINUTES	MED/HIGH	**20** MINUTES

2 pieces lamb rib roast
  each with 6 ribs, with
  backbone removed
salt
2 tablespoons lime marmalade
½ lb small new potatoes
½ lb baby carrots
10 oz frozen snow peas
For the lime dressing:
2 tablespoons butter

1 tablespoon lime marmalade
1 tablespoon fresh lime juice
½ teaspoon chopped fresh mint
pepper
For the garnish:
8 thin slices lime, for lime twists
1 mint sprig
French rib frills

Serves 4

1 To shape the crown, remove the fell from the fatty side of the lamb and remove the fat and meat from the bone ends. Cut away the gristle and meat in between and scrape the bone ends clean. Season the lamb lightly with salt.

2 On the meaty side of the lamb, make slits in between each rib base. Sew the lamb together with the fat inside, then bend it around to form a ring and sew together. Weigh the roast and calculate the cooking time at 10 minutes per 1 lb.

3 Cover the exposed pieces of bone with small smooth strips of foil. (Check your oven handbook to make sure you can use foil in your oven in this way.) Fill the center of the crown with crumpled waxed paper and place upside-down on a microwave roasting rack in the oven. Microwave at 50% (medium) for half the calculated time.

4 Place 2 tablespoons lime marmalade in a small bowl and microwave at 100% (high) for about 1 minute to melt.

5 Remove the waxed paper from the center of the roast, turn up the right way and brush the meat all over with the marmalade. Return to the oven and cook at 100% (high) for the remaining time.

6 Cover the lamb with a "tent" of foil and let stand for 20 minutes. Place the potatoes in a single layer in a shallow dish, add ¼ cup water, cover with pierced plastic wrap and microwave at 100% (high) for 3 minutes. Add the carrots, re-cover and microwave at 100% (high) for 8 minutes. Add the snow peas, re-cover and cook on 100% (high) for a further 4 minutes. Drain well.

7 To make the dressing, place the butter and marmalade in a bowl and microwave at 100% (high) for about 1 minute to melt. Stir in the lime juice, mint and pepper to taste. Pour over the

vegetables and stir carefully to coat.

8 Transfer the lamb to a large serving dish and remove the foil. Spoon some of the vegetables into the center of the crown and arrange the remainder around the base.

9 Place a frill on the end of each bone. Arrange lime twists around the base and serve, carved into ribs.

LAMB & PASTA MEDLEY

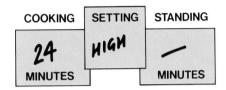

COOKING	SETTING	STANDING
24 MINUTES	HIGH	— MINUTES

1 tablespoon olive oil
1 onion, chopped
1 green pepper, seeded and chopped
2 zucchini, minced
1 lb ground raw lamb
1 can (16 oz) tomatoes
1¼ cups boiling water
2 cups pasta shapes
½ teaspoon dried basil
½ teaspoon dried thyme
salt and pepper
1 cup sliced mushrooms
grated Parmesan cheese, for garnish

Serves 4

1 Place the oil in a 2 quart casserole with the onion, green pepper and zucchini, and microwave at 100% (high) for 3 minutes.

2 Add the lamb, and microwave at 100% (high) for 5 minutes, stirring 2-3 times to remove any lumps. Pour off any excess fat.

3 Stir in tomatoes with their juice and the boiling water, breaking them up with a spoon. Cover and microwave at 100% (high) for 5 minutes.

4 Add the pasta, herbs and salt and pepper to taste and mix well. Re-cover and microwave at 100% (high) for 6 minutes.

5 Stir in the mushrooms and cook at 100% (high) for 5 minutes, uncovered. Serve at once, sprinkled with Parmesan cheese.

Lamb & Pasta Medley

ROAST LAMB WITH ORANGE & MINT

COOKING	SETTING	STANDING
25 MINUTES	HIGH/MED	15 MINUTES

2 lb fillet end leg of lamb
1 clove garlic, sliced in thin
  slivers
⅔ cup fresh orange juice
2 tablespoons bottled mint jelly
salt and pepper
2 tablespoons margarine or
  butter
¼ cup cup all-purpose flour
1¼ cups hot chicken stock
mint sprigs and orange slices,
  for garnish

Serves 4

1 Using a sharp knife, score the lamb fat diagonally, to make a diamond pattern. Make a few slits in the lamb and press a sliver of garlic into each one.
2 Weigh the lamb and calculate the exact cooking time as follows: 9-10 minutes per 1 lb for rare: 11-12 minutes per 1 lb for medium; 13-14 minutes per lb for well-done lamb. Place the lamb in a shallow bowl.
3 In a separate bowl, combine the orange juice, mint jelly, salt and pepper. Spoon the mixture over the lamb, cover loosely, chill, and let marinate for 6-8 hours, or overnight, turning and basting occasionally.
4 Place the lamb dish in the oven and microwave at 100% (high) for 5 minutes. Reduce the power to 50% (medium) for the remaining time and cook, turning meat over halfway through, and basting occasionally with the marinade. Test with a microwave thermometer for doneness if wished.

5 Drain off the marinade juices and reserve, skim off any excess fat. Cover the meat in its dish loosely with foil and let stand for 15 minutes, to finish cooking.
6 Place the margarine in a bowl, and microwave at 100% (high) for 1 minute to melt. Sprinkle in the flour and mix. Gradually stir in the stock and reserved marinade. Microwave at 100% (high) for 2-3 minutes, or until thick, stirring 2-3 times. Add salt and pepper to taste.
7 Slice the lamb and serve garnished with mint and orange slices. Pass the sauce in a sauceboat separately.

LAMB WITH ROSEMARY

COOKING	SETTING	STANDING
48 MINUTES	HIGH/MED	— MINUTES

3-3½ lb loin end of leg of lamb
2 cloves garlic, cut in slivers
3 sprigs of fresh rosemary or
  ½ tablespoon dried
  rosemary
2 tablespoons olive oil
1 large onion, minced
2 cans (16 oz each) tomatoes
1 tablespoon sugar (optional)
finely grated rind of ½ lemon
salt and pepper
rosemary sprigs, for garnish

Serves 4-6

1 Weigh the lamb and calculate the cooking time as follows: 9-10 minutes per 1 lb for rare; 11-12 minutes per 1 lb for medium; 13-14 minutes per 1 lb for well done.
2 Using a small sharp knife, make ½ inch deep slits all over the surface of the lamb. Push a garlic sliver and a few rosemary leaves, or a tiny pinch of dried rosemary, deep into alternate slits.
3 Place a browning dish in the

Lamb with Rosemary

oven and preheat at 100% (high) for 5 minutes. Add 1 tablespoon oil and the lamb and microwave at 100% (high) for 3-4 minutes, turning 2-3 times to brown the meat on all sides. Set aside.

4 Place the remaining oil and the onion in a 3 quart casserole and microwave at 100% (high) for 3 minutes, stirring twice. Add the tomatoes with their juice, the sugar, if using, and the lemon rind. Return to the oven and microwave at 100% (high) for 3 minutes. Break up the tomatoes with a wooden spoon and add salt and pepper to taste.

5 Add the lamb to the casserole and baste with the tomato sauce. Cover tightly and microwave at 100% (high) for 5 minutes. Reduce to 50% (medium) for the remaining calculated cooking time. Turn the lamb once, midway through the cooking time, to ensure it is evenly cooked.

6 Transfer the lamb to a warmed serving dish and let stand. Microwave the tomato sauce at 100% (high) for 5-6 minutes, uncovered, stirring occasionally, until the sauce has reduced and thickened to the consistency of ketchup.

7 Carve the lamb in thick slices and arrange on an oval serving platter. Pour over some of the sauce. Garnish with sprigs of rosemary and serve immediately. Pour the remaining sauce into a warmed sauceboat and serve with the lamb.

PORTUGUESE PORK

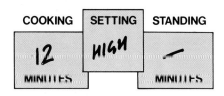

COOKING	SETTING	STANDING
12 MINUTES	HIGH	— MINUTES

1 large grapefruit
1½ lb pork tenderloin, sliced in thin strips

Portuguese Pork

2 teaspoons ground coriander pepper
¼ cup dry white wine
1 tablespoon tomato paste
1 jar (6 oz) pimientos, drained and cut in strips
sprig of watercress, for garnish

Serves 4

1 Grate the rind from the grapefruit and reserve. Remove all the remaining rind and pith, then divide the flesh in sections, cutting away all membranes.

2 Put the strips of pork in a bowl, sprinkle with the ground coriander, the grated rind of the grapefruit and pepper to taste and turn the meat until it is thoroughly coated.

3 Place a large microwave browning dish in the oven and preheat at 100% (high) for 5 minutes. Add the pork, cover and microwave at 100% (high) for 5 minutes, stirring twice.

4 Place one fourth of the grapefruit sections in a strainer set over a bowl and press with a wooden spoon to extract all the juice. Add the juice to the meat

and stir in the wine, tomato paste and pimientos. Microwave at 100% (high) for 3-4 minutes, uncovered, stirring twice.

5 Transfer the pork and pimientos to a warmed serving dish with a slotted spoon.

6 Microwave the liquid in the dish at 100% (high) for 3 minutes, uncovered. Add the remaining grapefruit sections and microwave at 100% (high) for 1 minute.

7 Remove the grapefruit sections from the dish with a slotted spoon and reserve. Pour the juices over the pork and pimientos, then garnish with the reserved grapefruit sections and the sprig of watercress. Serve at once.

M·I·C·R·O·T·I·P

A microwaved joint will keep its heat longer than a conventionally cooked joint. Tented in foil, it will stay hot for 30-40 minutes, while accompanying vegetables are cooked in the microwave.

CRISPY STUFFED HAM

COOKING	SETTING	STANDING
28 MINUTES	HIGH	— MINUTES

3 lb rolled ham roast,
    tied with string
2 teaspoons dried rosemary
2 bay leaves
For the stuffing:
3 tablespoons margarine or
    butter
2 cups soft white bread
    crumbs
1 tablespoon chopped fresh
    thyme or 1 ½ teaspoons
    dried thyme
grated rind of 1 lemon
chopped flesh of ½ lemon
pepper
beaten egg, to bind
For the coating:
1 ½ cups soft brown bread
    crumbs
¾ cup shredded Cheddar
    cheese
2 tablespoons chopped fresh
    parsley

Serves 6

1 Place the ham in a large bowl, cover with cold water and let soak overnight to remove the excess salt.
2 Drain the ham roast and place in a roasting bag with the rosemary and bay leaves. Prick the bag and secure with a non-metallic tag. Place in a shallow dish and microwave at 100% (high) for 10 minutes.
3 To make the stuffing, mix all the ingredients together in a bowl, adding enough egg to bind.
4 Remove the ham from the bag, and remove the string. Loosen the rind with a knife and peel it off. Spread the stuffing in the center of the roast and roll or fold it up again. Tie securely with string in several places.
5 Place on a roasting rack, cover with waxed paper and microwave at 100% (high) for 15 minutes.
6 Meanwhile, to make the coating, place the bread crumbs, cheese and parsley in a bowl and mix thoroughly.
7 Remove the ham from the oven and press the coating firmly over the surface. Return to the oven and microwave, uncovered, at 100% (high) for 3 minutes, or until the meat juices run clear when the roast is pierced in the center with a skewer. Transfer the ham to a heatproof plate and place under a preheated broiler to brown the coating.
8 Serve hot or cold, cut in fairly thick slices. Remove the string from the ham as you carve.

ORANGE HAM STEAKS

COOKING	SETTING	STANDING
13 MINUTES	HIGH/MED	— MINUTES

6 pickled onions, chopped
1 tablespoon light brown
    sugar
½ teaspoon ground mace
pepper
4 ham steaks, ¼ lb each,
    rinded
1 large orange
⅔ cup chicken stock
parsley sprigs, for garnish

Serves 4

Orange Ham Steaks

1 In a bowl, mix the pickled onions with the sugar, mace and pepper to taste.

2 Arrange the ham steaks in a single layer in a shallow serving dish or casserole. Cut the orange in 8 slices, working over the serving dish to catch as much juice as possible. Put 2 orange slices on each steak. Sprinkle the sugar mixture evenly over the ham, then add the stock so that the ham steaks are steeped in the stock and orange juice mixture.

3 Cover loosely with pierced plastic wrap and microwave at 100% (high) for 8-10 minutes, turning the dish after 5 minutes. Reduce to 50% (medium) and microwave for 5 minutes more. Garnish with parsley sprigs and serve immediately.

Ginger Ham Steaks

GINGER HAM STEAKS

COOKING	SETTING	STANDING
13	*HIGH*	*—*
MINUTES		MINUTES

4 ham steaks (about 6 oz each)
1 tablespoon margarine or
*   butter*
2 onions, thinly sliced
1 tablespoon cornstarch
1 can (16 oz) tomatoes
⅓ cup preserved gingerroot,
*   cut in thin strips*
¼ cup ginger syrup or honey
salt and pepper
parsley sprigs, for garnish

Serves 4

1 With a sharp pair of kitchen shears, snip the fat around the edge of the ham steaks at ½ inch intervals to prevent curling.

2 Arrange the steaks as far as possible in a single layer on a large plate. Cover with paper towels and microwave at 100% (high) for 8-9 minutes, rearrang-ing the steaks midway through the cooking time.

3 Place the margarine and onions in a 1 quart bowl and microwave at 100% (high) for 2 minutes. In a small bowl, mix the cornstarch with 2 tablespoons of the tomato juice from the can to make a smooth paste.

4 Add the tomatoes with the re-maining can juices and the pre-seved ginger and ginger syrup to the onions in the dish. Stir in the cornstarch paste, mixing well. Microwave at 100% (high) for 3-4 minutes, or until boiling. Add salt and pepper to taste.

5 Transfer the ham steaks to a warmed serving dish, letting them overlap slightly, then spoon over the sauce. Garnish the steaks with parsley sprigs and serve at once.

CREAMY HAM & SPAGHETTI

COOKING	SETTING	STANDING
11	*HIGH*	*6*
MINUTES		MINUTES

5 cups boiling water
1 tablespoon vegetable oil
1 lb spaghetti
⅔ cup light cream
1 cup diced ham
4 tomatoes, peeled and diced
1 cup thinly sliced mushrooms
salt and pepper
1 tablespoon minced fresh
*   parsley*

Serves 6

1 Place the boiling water in a large bowl with the oil. Mic-rowave at 100% (high) for 2 minutes. Add the spaghetti to the bowl, pressing it down as it sof-tens until it is totally submerged. Stir thoroughly. Cover with pierced plastic wrap.

2 Microwave at 100% (high) for 6 minutes, stirring after 3 minutes. Let it stand for 5 minutes.

3 Drain the spaghetti completely and stir in the cream together with all the remaining ingre-dients, except the parsley. Cover with pierced plastic wrap and microwave at 100% (high) for 3 minutes. Allow to stand for 1 minute. Stir in the minced parsley and serve immediately.

Beef Curry with Rice Pilaf

BEEF CURRY WITH RICE PILAF

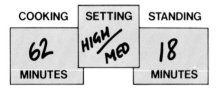

COOKING	SETTING	STANDING
62 MINUTES	HIGH/MED	18 MINUTES

1 tablespoon vegetable oil
1 large onion, chopped
2 teaspoons ground coriander
½ teaspoon ground cumin
½ teaspoon chili seasoning
1 teaspoon ground cardamom
1 inch piece gingerroot, pared
    and finely chopped
1 tablespoon tomato paste
1¼ lb top round steak, cut in 1
    inch cubes
¼ cup all-purpose flour, sifted
    with ½ teaspoon turmeric
2 cups hot beef stock
For the garnish:
coriander leaves
grated fresh coconut
    (optional)
For the rice pilaf:
1 cup long-grain rice, well
    washed and drained
2 tablespoons butter
a few strands of saffron or

½ teaspoon turmeric
¼ teaspoon ground cardamom
¼ teaspoon ground cinnamon
salt

Serves 4

1 Put the oil, onion and spices into a large casserole and mix together. Microwave at 100% (high) for 4 minutes, stirring halfway through. Add the tomato paste and microwave at 100% (high) for 2 minutes.
2 Meanwhile, toss the steak cubes in the flour and turmeric. Add the steak to the onion mixture and microwave at 100% (high) for 5 minutes. Pour in the hot stock, cover, and microwave at 100% (high) for 5 minutes, or until boiling.
3 Reduce the power to 50% (medium) and microwave for 30-35 minutes. Stand for 13 minutes.
4 While the curry is standing, put the rice in a large bowl. Add the butter and microwave for 3-4 minutes, stirring after 2 minutes. Add 2½ cups boiling water, the saffron or turmeric, spices and salt. Cover with pierced plastic wrap and microwave at 100%

(high) for 10 minutes.
5 Let the rice stand for 5 minutes and microwave beef at 100% (high) for 3-4 minutes. Garnish with coriander and coconut, if liked.

MARINATED SUMMER BEEF

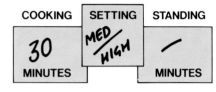

COOKING	SETTING	STANDING
30 MINUTES	MED/HIGH	— MINUTES

1½-2 lb beef round roast
1 small onion, finely sliced
For the marinade:
7 tablespoons vegetable oil
⅔ cup dry white wine
1 teaspoon Louisiana mustard
1 teaspoon dried thyme
1 tablespoon lemon juice
1 clove garlic, crushed (optional)
salt and pepper
For the salad:
1½ cups uncooked potato
    chunks
½ package (10 oz size) frozen
    green beans
2 carrots, grated
2 tomatoes, quartered
For the garnish:
10-12 pitted ripe olives
1 tablespoon chopped fresh
    parsley

Serves 4

1 Weigh the beef and calculate the cooking time at 10 minutes per 1 lb for rare. Increase to 12 minutes per 1 lb if meat is preferred medium done.
2 Place the meat on a roasting rack and cover with waxed paper or place on an inverted saucer in a roasting bag. Microwave at 50% (medium) for the calculated time, turning the roast over after half the cooking time. Remove the beef and let cool for about 45 minutes.
3 To make the marinade, put the

oil, wine, mustard, thyme, lemon juice and garlic, if using, in a bowl or in the goblet of a blender. Season with salt and pepper and beat well with a fork, or process in the blender for 30 seconds.

4 Slice the cooled beef into even, neat slices and arrange them in a shallow dish. Arrange the onion slices on top of the beef and pour over the marinade. Cover the dish with plastic wrap and refrigerate for at least 5-6 hours or overnight if possible.

5 To make the salad, place the potatoes in a 3 cup bowl with 2 tablespoons water. Cover with pierced plastic wrap and microwave at 100% (high) for 6 minutes, or until just tender. Drain well.

6 Place the beans in a 3 cup bowl with 2 tablespoons water. Cover with pierced plastic wrap and microwave at 100% (high) for 4 minutes. Drain well and mix with the potatoes. While the vegetables are still warm, pour over 2 tablespoons of the marinade from the beef. Toss gently with a fork to coat thoroughly with the

marinade, taking care not to break up the vegetables. Cover and chill in the refrigerator for 1 hour.

7 When ready to serve, mix the grated carrots and the tomatoes with the potatoes and beans. Remove the meat slices from the marinade, draining off any excess marinade. Remove the onions from the marinade with a slotted spoon and mix them into the salad.

8 Pile the vegetable salad into the center of a serving platter and arrange the beef slices around it. Garnish the platter with ripe olives and chopped parsley. Serve at once.

VINEYARD BEEF BRAISE

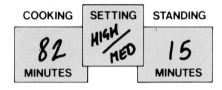

COOKING	SETTING	STANDING
82 MINUTES	HIGH/MED	15 MINUTES

2 tablespoons vegetable oil
2 celery stalks, thinly sliced

1 onion, thinly sliced
2 carrots, thinly sliced
3½ lb top round of beef
⅔ cup red wine
salt and pepper
2 garlic cloves, crushed
1 bouquet garni
For the sauce:
2 beef bouillon cubes
⅔ cup water
⅔ cup red wine
1 tablespoon soy sauce
2 teaspoons tomato paste
2 teaspoons cornstarch
a little water

Serves 6

1 Put the oil, celery, onion and carrots in a 3 quart casserole. Cover with pierced plastic wrap and microwave at 100% (high) for 8 minutes, stirring once.

2 Arrange the beef on top of the vegetables. Add the wine, salt, pepper, garlic and the bouquet garni. Re-cover and microwave at 50% (medium) for 35 minutes.

3 Turn the meat over. Replace the wrap and microwave at 50% (medium) for a further 35 minutes. Turn over again, cover: let stand for 15 minutes.

4 Remove meat and wrap it in foil to keep warm.

5 Remove the vegetables using a slotted spoon and discard. Reserve the cooking juices.

6 Pour off excess fat, then add the bouillon cubes to the remaining liquid. Stir in the water, wine, soy sauce and tomato paste. Microwave at 100% (high) for 2-3 minutes, stirring once.

7 Mix the cornstarch with a little water until smooth, then stir it into the sauce. Cover with pierced plastic wrap and microwave at 100% (high) for 2 minutes, stirring once or twice until smooth and thick.

8 Slice the beef and arrange it on a heated serving platter with a little of the sauce. Serve immediately with the rest of the sauce passed separately.

Marinated Summer Beef

BISTRO BEEF

COOKING	SETTING	STANDING
79 MINUTES	HIGH/LOW	— MINUTES

¼ cup all-purpose flour
salt and pepper
1½ lb beef top round,
  trimmed and cut in
  1 inch cubes
2 tablespoons beef drippings
2 onions, sliced
1 clove garlic, crushed
2 carrots, sliced
1¼ cups red wine

1¼ cups beef stock
4 tablespoons tomato paste
bouquet garni
For the topping:
4 chunky slices French bread
1-2 tablespoons Dijon mustard

Serves 4

1 Put the flour in a plastic bag and season with salt and pepper. Place the meat in the bag and shake until the meat is well coated with flour. Reserve any excess flour.
2 Place the drippings in a 2 quart casserole, add the onions, garlic and carrots, and microwave at 100% (high) for 5 minutes, stirring twice. Remove the vegetables with a slotted spoon and set aside.
3 Add the meat to the fat remaining in the casserole and microwave at 100% (high) for 5 minutes. Return the vegetables to the casserole and stir in any reserved flour.
4 Gradually blend in the red wine, beef stock and tomato paste. Add the bouquet garni and salt and pepper to taste.
5 Cover and microwave at 100% (high) for 8 minutes. Reduce to 30% (low) and microwave for 1 hour, stirring 4-5 times. Remove the bouquet garni.
6 Spread the French bread with mustard and arrange, mustard side up, on top of the casserole. Return to the oven, and cook, uncovered, at 100% (high) for 1 minute to warm the bread.

Bistro Beef

MEATBALLS WITH WALNUTS

COOKING	SETTING	STANDING
22½ MINUTES	HIGH	5 MINUTES

1 tablespoon vegetable oil
1 cup chopped walnuts

Meatballs with Walnuts

½ cup milk
2 slices wholewheat bread,
  crusts removed
1½ lb lean ground beef
1 egg, beaten
grated rind and juice of ½ lemon
salt and pepper
1 tablespoon margarine or
  butter
1 tablespoon all-purpose flour
1¼ hot beef stock
2 tablespoons heavy cream
walnut halves and lemon twists,
  for garnish

For the noodles:
½ lb egg noodles
1 tablespoon vegetable oil
1 teaspoon salt

Serves 4-6

1 To cook the noodles, place the noodles, oil and salt in a large deep bowl. Add 1 quart boiling water to cover the noodles. Cover the bowl with pierced plastic wrap and microwave at 100% (high) for 6 minutes. Let stand, covered for 5 minutes, then drain.

2 Place the oil and nuts in a bowl and microwave at 100% (high) for 2-3 minutes. Remove with a slotted spoon and drain well on paper towels.

3 Transfer three-quarters of the nuts to a large bowl. Reserve the remaining chopped nuts. Put the milk in a separate shallow bowl and add the bread. Press the bread down well with a fork to absorb the milk. Break up the soaked bread with the fork and add to the large bowl containing the ground nuts.

4 Add the ground beef, egg, lemon rind and juice and stir thoroughly to mix. Add salt and pepper to taste. Divide in 24 pieces and, using floured hands, shape into balls.

5 Place half the meatballs around the edge of a large round dish, with a gap between each one. Microwave at 100% (high) for 3-4 minutes, turning over and rearranging after 2 minutes. Place on paper towels. Cook remaining meatballs in the same way at 100% (high) for 3-4 minutes, turning after 2 minutes.

6 Place the margarine in a 4 cup measure and microwave at 100% (high) for 20-30 seconds to melt. Stir in the flour. Gradually mix in the stock, and microwave at 100% (high) for 2 minutes, or until thick, stirring 2-3 times.

7 Mix the meatball batches together and pour the sauce over the top. Cover with pierced plastic wrap and microwave at 100% (high) for 5 minutes, turning the dish after 3 minutes. Stir in the cream and reserved chopped walnuts.

8 Arrange the noodles around the edge of a serving platter, cover with pierced plastic wrap and microwave for 1 minute to reheat. Pour the sauce and meatballs in the center and serve, garnished with walnut halves and lemon twists.

CRUNCH BURGERS

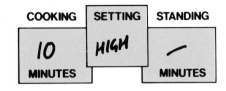

COOKING	SETTING	STANDING
10 MINUTES	HIGH	— MINUTES

1 ½ lb ground beef
1 onion, minced
½ cup chopped salted peanuts
1 egg, beaten
salt and pepper
5 bacon slices
Accompaniments:
6 lettuce leaves
6 sesame buns, split
6 teaspoons mayonnaise
3 tomatoes, sliced
4 inch piece of cucumber,
*   pared and thinly sliced*

Serves 6

1 Break up the ground beef, using 2 knives.
2 Mix the ground beef with the onion, peanuts, egg, salt and pepper. Form into 6 burgers of equal size and leave, covered, in the refrigerator.
3 Arrange the bacon on a plate covered with a paper towel. Place 1 more paper towel on top of the bacon. Microwave at 100% (high) for 5-6 minutes or until crisp. Crumble the bacon well and set it aside.
4 Preheat a browning dish for 5 minutes according to the manufacturer's directions. Add the burgers to the dish and microwave at 100% (high) for 3 minutes on one side, then for 2 minutes on the second side.
5 Place a lettuce leaf on the bottom half of each bun. Top it with a burger and add a generous spoonful of mayonnaise. Sprinkle the mayonnaise with crumbled bacon and finally add tomato and cucumber slices. Assemble the remaining cruchburgers in the same way and replace the bun lids. Serve.

Crunch Burgers

VEAL CHOPS WITH TOMATO SAUCE

COOKING	SETTING	STANDING
17 MINUTES	HIGH	— MINUTES

4 veal chops, total weight
   1½ lb
1 onion, chopped
1 teaspoon dried oregano
½ teaspoon dried basil
2 tablespoons butter
¼ cup all-purpose flour
1 can (16 oz) chopped
   tomatoes
2 tablespoons tomato paste
salt and pepper
For the garnish:
pitted ripe olives
2 tablespoons chopped fresh
   parsley

Serves 4

1 Place a microwave browning dish in the oven and preheat at 100% (high) for 5 minutes. Place the chops in the dish, cover and microwave at 100% (high) for 4 minutes. Turn the chops over and cook at 100% (high) for a further 3-4 minutes, or until brown on both sides.
2 Place the onion, oregano, basil and butter in a 2 quart casserole and microwave at 100% (high) for 2 minutes. Stir in the flour, tomatoes with their juice, tomato paste and season to taste.
3 Return the casserole to the oven and microwave at 100% (high) for 5-6 minutes, stirring 2-3 times, or until smooth and thick.
4 Place the chops on a serving dish, pour over the sauce and cover with pierced plastic wrap. Microwave at 100% (high) for 3-4 minutes.
5 Garnish with ripe olives and herbs and serve at once.

Veal Chops with Tomato Sauce

VEAL WITH LEMON HOLLANDAISE

COOKING	SETTING	STANDING
8 MINUTES	HIGH/MED	— MINUTES

6 veal scallops, weighing about
   ¼ lb each
pepper
2 tablespoons butter
For the sauce:
½ cup butter
2 tablespoons lemon
   juice
½ teaspoon dry mustard
2 egg yolks
salt and white pepper
For the garnish:
fresh mint leaves
lemon slices

Serves 6

1 To make the sauce, place the butter in a large measuring cup and microwave at 100% (high) for 1½ minutes. Mix in the lemon juice, mustard and egg yolks. Beat well and add salt and pepper to taste. Cook at 50% (medium) for 1 minute to thicken. Do not let boil.
2 Place a large microwave browning dish in the oven and preheat at 100% (high) for 5 minutes.
3 Season the veal scallops with pepper. Place the butter and 3 scallops in the browning dish and microwave at 100% (high) for 2½-3½ minutes. Turn the scallops over after 2 minutes. Repeat with the remaining 3 scallops.
4 Arrange the veal on a serving platter. Microwave the sauce at 100% (high) for 30 seconds to heat. Do not overheat as it may curdle. Pour the sauce over the veal, garnish with mint leaves and slices of lemon and serve at once.

49

LEMON LIVER

COOKING	SETTING	STANDING
15 MINUTES	HIGH / MED	— MINUTES

2 tablespoons margarine or
  butter
1 ½ lb calf liver, thinly sliced
  and cut in 1 inch pieces
1 large onion, chopped
1 can (16 oz) chopped
  tomatoes
finely grated rind of 1 small
  lemon
2 tablespoons tomato paste
2 teaspoons Dijon mustard
⅓ cup pitted ripe olives
salt and pepper
Accompaniments:
⅓ cup pitted ripe olives,
  chopped
grated rind of 1 small
  lemon
2 cups pasta shapes,
  cooked (optional)

Serves 4

1 Place a large microwave browning dish in the oven and preheat at 100% (high) for 5 minutes. Add the margarine and liver. Cover and microwave at 100% (high) for 5 minutes, stirring after 2 minutes. Add the onion and microwave at 100% (high) for 2 minutes.
2 Stir in the canned tomatoes with their juice, the lemon rind, tomato paste and mustard. Mix well to blend all the ingredients, then add the ripe olives.
3 Microwave at 100% (high) for 3 minutes, then reduce the power to 50% (medium) and cook for a further 5 minutes.
4 Season to taste with salt and pepper and transfer to a warmed serving dish. Sprinkle over the chopped olives and grated lemon rind and serve at once, while hot. If wished, serve on a bed of pasta.

Italian-Style Kidneys

ITALIAN-STYLE KIDNEYS

COOKING	SETTING	STANDING
9 MINUTES	HIGH	— MINUTES

1 ¼ lb lamb kidneys, skinned
  halved and cored
3 tablespoons butter
1 tablespoon vegetable oil
1 clove garlic, halved
1 cup thinly sliced button
  mushrooms
2 tablespoons lemon
  juice
salt and pepper
1 cup long-grain rice, cooked
  and drained
For the garnish:
chopped fresh parsley
parsley sprigs
lemon wedges

Serves 4

1 Pat the kidneys dry with paper towels. Place 2 tablespoons butter, the oil, garlic and kidneys in a 2 quart casserole. Microwave at 100% (high) for 5-6 minutes, stirring 2-3 times, or until kidneys are cooked.
2 Using a slotted spoon, transfer the kidneys to a plate. Discard the garlic. Cut each kidney crosswise in 4-5 slices and return to the casserole.
3 Place the remaining butter in a small casserole, add the sliced mushrooms, microwave at 100% (high) for 2 minutes, then stir. Add to the kidneys with the lemon juice.
4 Season to taste with salt and pepper, stir and microwave at 100% (high) for 2-3 minutes, to heat through.
5 Spread the hot rice onto a warmed serving platter, spoon the kidney mixture on top, garnish with chopped parsley, parsley sprigs and lemon wedges and serve.

KIDNEYS IN CIDER

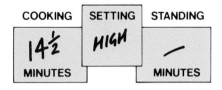

COOKING	SETTING	STANDING
14½ MINUTES	HIGH	— MINUTES

1 cup pearl onions, unpeeled
1¼ lb lamb kidneys, skinned, halved and cored
2 tablespoons margarine or butter
1 cup small button mushrooms
2 bacon slices, cut in thin strips
2 tablespoons all-purpose flour
1 cup hard cider or dry white wine
1 tablespoon tomato paste
1 bay leaf
salt and pepper
1 tablespoon minced fresh parsley, for garnish
toast triangles, to serve

Serves 4

1 Place the onions in a 1 quart bowl with 3 tablespoons water, cover with pierced plastic wrap and microwave at 100% (high) for 4 minutes. Peel the onions and use a sharp knife to trim the root ends and tops.
2 Pat the kidneys dry with paper towels.
3 Place the margarine in a 2 quart casserole and microwave at 100% (high) for 30 seconds to melt. Add the onions and mushrooms and microwave at 100% (high) for 2 minutes. Add the kidneys and bacon and microwave at 100% (high) for 3 minutes, stirring the mixture twice during the cooking time.
4 Stir in the flour. Gradually add the cider and tomato paste, mixing well. Add the bay leaf. Cover with casserole lid or pierced plastic wrap and microwave at 100% (high) for 5 minutes, stirring 2-3 times. Season with salt and pepper to taste.
5 Transfer the kidneys in their sauce to a warmed serving dish, discard the bay leaf, sprinkle with parsley and serve with toast triangles.

Kidneys in Cider

TAGLIATELLE & CHICKEN LIVERS

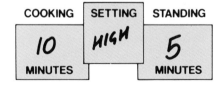

COOKING	SETTING	STANDING
10 MINUTES	HIGH	5 MINUTES

1 tablespoon vegetable oil
¾ lb fresh tagliatelle
1 tablespoon butter
1 small onion, minced
1 clove garlic, crushed
1 green pepper, seeded and sliced
½ lb chicken livers, trimmed, each liver halved
1 cup sliced mushrooms
3 tablespoons chopped fresh parsley
3 tomatoes, cut in wedges
salt and pepper
grated Parmesan, for garnish

Serves 4

1 Place 7½ cups boiling water in a bowl with the oil. Microwave at 100% (high) for 2 minutes. Add tagliatelle, cover and microwave at 100% (high) for 4-5 minutes. Stir, re-cover and stand for 5 minutes.
2 Meanwhile place the butter in a shallow casserole with the onion, garlic, green pepper and chicken livers. Cover with pierced plastic wrap and microwave at 100% (high) for 3-3½ minutes, stirring once.
3 Drain pasta thoroughly and add the chicken liver mixture with the mushrooms, parsley, and tomatoes. Season to taste.
4 Cover with pierced plastic wrap. Microwave at 100% (high) for 1-2 minutes. Sprinkle with Parmesan and serve immediately.

P·O·U·L·T·R·Y A·N·D F·I·S·H

Roast Chicken with Yogurt

ROAST CHICKEN WITH YOGURT

COOKING	SETTING	STANDING
50 MINUTES	HIGH/MED	5 MINUTES

4 lb oven-ready roasting chicken, skinned, giblets removed and trussed
hot cooked rice
sprigs of fresh mint, for garnish
For the marinade:
1 clove garlic, crushed
2 tablespoons chopped fresh mint

1 tablespoon ground cumin
2 teaspoons sugar
1 teaspoon ground ginger
1 teaspoon salt
½ teaspoon chili powder
½ teaspoon turmeric
½ teaspoon ground allspice
1¼ cups plain yogurt

Serves 4-6

1 Wash the chicken and dry thoroughly with paper towels. Score it with a very sharp knife, then place the chicken in a large bowl.

2 To make the marinade, mix together all the marinade ingredients, pour over the chicken, cover and leave to marinate in the refrigerator, for at least 8 hours or overnight. Spoon the marinade over occasionally.

3 Place the chicken, breast-side down, on a roasting rack or inverted plate in a dish and pour over the marinade. Cover lightly with waxed paper and microwave at 100% (high) for 15 minutes. Turn chicken over, reduce power to 50% (medium) and microwave for 35-40 minutes or until the juices run clear when the flesh is pierced in the thickest part with a skewer. Give the dish a quarter turn every 10 minutes. Remove waxed paper for the last 20 minutes.

4 Let stand for 5-10 minutes. Serve on a warm dish, on a bed of rice, garnished with mint.

Chicken with Creamy Corn Sauce

CHICKEN WITH CREAMY CORN SAUCE

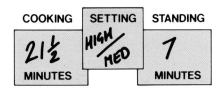

COOKING	SETTING	STANDING
21½ MINUTES	HIGH/MED	7 MINUTES

2 tablespoons butter
4 (½ lb) chicken pieces
salt and pepper
paprika
tomato wedges,
   for garnish
For the sauce:
1 small onion, minced
1 can (10 oz) whole kernel corn,
   drained
¼ cup all-purpose
   flour
1¼ cups milk

pinch of ground nutmeg
salt and pepper
2 tablespoons chopped fresh
   parsley

Serves 4

1 Put the butter in a bowl and microwave at 100% (high) for 20-30 seconds to melt.

2 Wipe the chicken portions with paper towels. Arrange in a single layer in a shallow dish with the thickest parts pointing out. Brush all over with butter, add salt and pepper, and dust with paprika.

3 Cover the chicken with pierced plastic wrap and microwave at 70% (medium high) for 8 minutes. Rearrange the chicken so the least cooked parts are nearest the outside. Re-cover with plastic wrap and microwave at 70% (medium high) for a further 6

minutes or until the chicken is tender and the juices run clear when the thickest part is pierced with a fine skewer.

4 Spoon off 2 tablespoons of the cooking juices into a 1½ quart bowl. Cover the chicken loosely with foil and let stand while you make the sauce.

5 To make the sauce, add the onion to the 1½ quart bowl and microwave at 100% (high) for 2 minutes until soft.

6 Stir in the corn and flour, then gradually add the milk and nutmeg until well mixed. Microwave at 100% (high) for 5 minutes, stirring 2-3 times, until thick. Season and stir in the parsley.

7 Arrange the chicken on a warmed serving platter. Spoon a little of the sauce over and pour the remainder into a warmed sauceboat. Garnish the chicken with tomato wedges and serve.

CASHEW CHICKEN

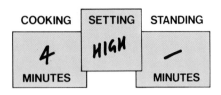

COOKING	SETTING	STANDING
4	*HIGH*	**—**
MINUTES		MINUTES

2 tablespoons soy sauce
2 tablespoons dry sherry
3 tablespoons oil
4 chicken breasts, skinned and
  cut in very thin strips
1 teaspoon cornstarch
1 clove garlic, crushed
1 inch piece fresh gingerroot
  pared and finely chopped
1 sweet red pepper, seeded and
  thinly sliced
¾ cup unsalted cashews
scallion curls, for garnish
  (optional)
Accompaniments (optional):
hot cooked rice
snow peas and scallions

Serves 4

1 Mix together the soy sauce,
sherry and 1 tablespoon oil.
Add the chicken strips and toss to
coat, then cover and let marinate
for 1 hour.
2 Drain the chicken pieces. Add
the marinade to the cornstarch
and mix to a paste.
3 Place a large microwave
browning dish in the oven and
preheat at 100% (high) for 5
minutes. Add the remaining oil
and chicken pieces and stir until
the sizzling stops.
4 Cover and microwave at 100%
(high) for 2 minutes. Add the
garlic, ginger, sweet red pepper,
nuts and thickened marinade and
stir well. Cover and microwave at
100% (high) for 2 minutes.
5 Arrange on a warmed serving
platter, garnish with scallion
curls, if liked, and serve. If
wished, serve this oriental dish
with plain boiled rice, and snow-
peas with scallions.

Cashew Chicken

MEDITERRANEAN STUFFED CHICKEN BREASTS

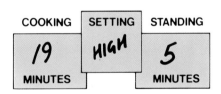

COOKING	SETTING	STANDING
19	*HIGH*	**5**
MINUTES		MINUTES

½ cup soft butter
juice of ½ lemon, strained
salt and pepper
1½ cups shelled shrimp, thawed
  if frozen
4 (6 oz) chicken breasts,
  skinned and boned
1 large onion, minced
2 cloves garlic, crushed
1 tablespoon vegetable oil
1 can (16 oz) tomatoes
2 chicken bouillon cubes
chopped fresh parsley, for
  garnish

Serves 4

1 Beat the butter with a little
lemon juice and salt and pepper.
Beat in three fourths of the
shrimp, reserving the remainder.
2 Make a long horizontal slit
through each chicken breast to
make a pocket. Fill the pocket
with the shrimp mixture, then
secure with wooden cocktail

picks to keep the filling enclosed. Place the chicken breasts in a large shallow heatproof dish and cover loosely with plastic wrap.

3 Put the onion, garlic and oil into a large casserole and mix well. Microwave at 100% (high) for 2 minutes, until softened.

4 Add the tomatoes with their juice, crumble in the bouillon cubes and season with salt and pepper. Cover the dish with pierced plastic wrap. Microwave at 100% (high) for 8 minutes, stirring twice. Set aside.

5 Microwave the chicken breasts at 100% (high) for 7-8 minutes, turning and rearranging them every 2 minutes. Remove, cover and let stand for 5 minutes.

6 Microwave the tomato sauce at 100% (high) for 2-3 minutes, or until boiling hot.

7 Arrange the chicken breasts on a hot serving dish, then spoon the tomato sauce over them. Garnish with the reserved shrimp and chopped parsley and serve immediately.

CHICKEN WITH PARSLEY DUMPLINGS

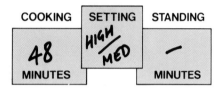

COOKING	SETTING	STANDING
48 MINUTES	HIGH/MED	— MINUTES

3 lb broiler-fryer
½ lemon
2½ cups hot chicken stock
2 large onions, sliced
2 carrots, sliced
2 celery stalks, sliced
1 teaspoon salt
a few sprigs of parsley
6-8 whole black peppercorns
parsley sprigs, for garnish
For the dumplings:
1 cup self-rising flour
¼ teaspoon salt
¼ cup shredded beef suet
1 tablespoon finely chopped fresh parsley
about ¼ cup milk
For the sauce:
2 tablespoons margarine
¼ cup all-purpose flour
⅔ cup milk

Serves 4-6

1 Wipe the chicken broiler-fryer inside and out with paper towels, then rub the skin all over with the cut lemon.

2 Put the chicken, breast-side down, in a large casserole. Add all the remaining ingredients except the parsley garnish. Microwave at 100% (high) for 5 minutes, then reduce the power to 50%

(medium) for 10 minutes. Turn the chicken over and microwave at 50% (medium) for a further 10 minutes.

3 Meanwhile, to make the dumplings, sift the flour and salt into a bowl and add the suet and parsley. Make a well in the center and add a little milk. Gradually work the dry ingredients into the center, adding just enough milk to make a firm dough. Divide the dough in 8 pieces and roll each into a ball with floured hands.

4 Add the dumplings to the casserole and microwave at 50% (medium) for a further 20 minutes.

5 Lift the chicken from the dish and drain it thoroughly. Pat dry with paper towels and then place on a warmed serving dish. Remove the dumplings with a slotted spoon and arrange them around the chicken.

6 Strain the cooking liquid left in the casserole and reserve ⅔ cup.

7 To make the sauce, place the margarine in a 4 cup liquid measure and microwave at 100% (high) for 30 seconds, or until melted. Sprinkle in the flour, then gradually stir in the milk and reserved cooking liquid. Microwave at 100% (high) for about 2½ minutes, stirring 2-3 times, or until thick and smooth.

8 Spoon a little of the sauce over the chicken and garnish with parsley sprigs. Serve at once, with the remaining sauce in a warmed sauceboat.

M·I·C·R·O·T·I·P

Fresh herbs may be dried in the microwave oven. Lay leaves or sprigs between sheets of paper towels and microwave at 100% (high) for 3-4 minutes, turning once, and watching carefully. When thoroughly dry, crumble and store in an airtight jar.

GOLDEN TURKEY WITH NOODLES

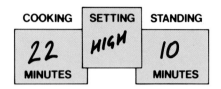

COOKING	SETTING	STANDING
22 MINUTES	HIGH	10 MINUTES

1 tablespoon oil
½ lb green egg noodles
salt
3 slices bacon, diced
¼ cup butter
minced fresh parsley,
   for garnish
For the sauce:
3 tablespoons butter
1 large onion, minced
1 large sweet pepper, seeded
   and cut in thin strips
1 clove garlic, crushed
1 lb turkey cutlets, cut
   in strips
⅓ cup all-purpose flour
⅔ cup hot chicken stock
1¼ cups hard cider or
   dry white wine
½ of a 10 oz package frozen
   whole kernel corn
½ teaspoon dried thyme
pepper
3 tablespoons light cream

Serves 4

1 Put the oil and noodles in a large bowl. Add salt to taste, then add 4 cups boiling water to cover the noodles. Cover the bowl with pierced plastic wrap and microwave at 100% (high) for 6 minutes. Let stand, covered, for 10 minutes while you prepare the rest of the dish.
2 For the sauce, combine the butter, onion, pepper and garlic in a large bowl. Cover the bowl and microwave at 100% (high) for 3 minutes.
3 Add the turkey to the bowl, cover and microwave at 100% (high) for 5 minutes. Stir after 2 minutes.
4 Gradually blend in the flour,

stock and cider or wine. Add the corn and thyme and season with salt and pepper. Microwave at 100% (high) for 5 minutes, stirring midway through cooking time. Add cream and stir so that all the ingredients are blended.
5 Place the bacon between two sheets of paper towels and microwave at 100% (high) for 2 minutes.
6 Place the butter in a small bowl and microwave at 100% (high) for 45-60 seconds, or until the butter melts.
7 Drain the noodles, pour over the melted butter, toss well, and spoon around the edge of a warmed dish.
8 Pour the turkey mixture into the center of the dish and sprinkle with the bacon. Garnish with the parsley and serve.

Duck with Olives

DUCK WITH OLIVES

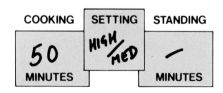

COOKING	SETTING	STANDING
50 MINUTES	HIGH/MED	— MINUTES

4 (¾ lb) duck pieces
1 onion, chopped
1 tablespoon tomato paste
½ teaspoon dried thyme
½ teaspoon dried rosemary
1 bay leaf
pepper
1¼ cups dry white wine
½ lb mushrooms, halved
1¼ cups pitted green
   olives

Serves 4

1 Wipe duck with paper towels, then make diagonal cuts on skin to form a diamond pattern.

2 Place the onion in a large casserole, cover and microwave at 100% (high) for 2 minutes.

3 Stir in tomato paste, thyme, rosemary, bay leaf, pepper and wine.

4 Add duck portions, cover and microwave at 100% (high) for 15 minutes, rearranging once.

5 Add the mushrooms and olives, cover and microwave at 50% (medium) for 30 minutes; stir once.

6 Remove duck and place under a preheated hot broiler. Broil for 1-2 minutes until skin goes crisp and brown. Arrange on warm serving platter with the olives and mushrooms.

7 Remove fat from the sauce, then microwave at 100% (high) for 3 minutes. Discard the bay leaf. Transfer the sauce to a sauceboat, and serve at once with the crispy duck and the olives and mushrooms.

CORNISH GAME HENS WITH GRAPES

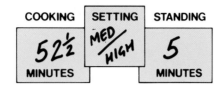

COOKING	SETTING	STANDING
52½ MINUTES	MED/HIGH	5 MINUTES

6 Cornish game hens, weighing about ¾ lb each
softened butter
For the stuffing:
4 chicken livers, chopped
⅓ cup chopped cooked ham
1 ⅓ cups cooked long-grain rice
½ teaspoon dried thyme
½ teaspoon dried oregano
1 large egg, beaten
salt and pepper
For the Hollandaise sauce:
1 cup butter
4 egg yolks
2 tablespoons lemon juice
1 teaspoon dry mustard
salt and pepper
For the garnish:
½ lb seedless white grapes, divided into small bunches
sprigs of fresh watercress or parsley

Serves 6

1 Clean the game hens and pat dry. Combine all the ingredients for the stuffing and loosely pack one sixth of the mixture into each hen. Truss the ends with small wooden or bamboo skewers to prevent the stuffing from falling out during cooking.

2 Generously spread each Cornish game hen with softened butter. Arrange the buttered hens breast down, in a ring, in a large baking dish.

3 Microwave at 70% (medium high) for 25 minutes. Turn hens breast side up. Spread with more butter. Microwave at 70% (medium high) for 25 minutes more or until the hens are tender and the juices run clear when the thighs are pierced with a fine skewer. Remove the hens from the microwave oven, cover loosely with foil and let stand while you make the Hollandaise sauce.

4 To make the sauce, place the butter in a glass measuring cup and microwave at 100% (high) for 2½-3½ minutes until hot and bubbly. Place remaining ingredients in a blender or food processor. Work for a few seconds, then add butter slowly through the feeder tube or lid, mixing until the sauce is thick and creamy.

5 Remove the wooden skewers from the Cornish game hens and arrange them on a large heated platter. Spoon a little of the Hollandaise sauce over each hen. Garnish with grapes and sprigs of watercress and serve immediately. Pass the remaining Hollandaise sauce separately in a small bowl.

Cornish Game Hens with Grapes

HALITBUT SPECIAL

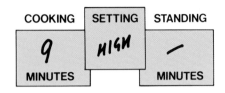

COOKING	SETTING	STANDING
9 MINUTES	HIGH	— MINUTES

4 halibut steaks, weighing
   about 6 oz each,
   skinned
⅔ cup dry white wine
1 tablespoon cornstarch
1 tablespoon cold water

For the topping:
2 tablespoon butter
1 onion, chopped
2 celery stalks, chopped
3 tomatoes, peeled and
   chopped
1 cup chopped mushrooms
1 teaspoon chopped fresh
   thyme or ½ teaspoon
   dried thyme
salt and pepper
For the garnish:
chopped fresh parsley
sprig of fresh thyme

Serves 4

Halibut Special

1 To make the topping, place the butter in a medium-size bowl. Add the onion and microwave at 100% (high) for 2 minutes.
2 Add the celery, tomatoes and mushrooms and microwave at 100% (high) for 1 further minute, stirring once or twice. Add the thyme, stir in salt and pepper to taste and set aside.
3 Arrange the halibut steaks in a single layer in a shallow dish. Spoon the vegetables over the halibut and pour the wine around. Cover with pierced plastic wrap and microwave at 100% (high) for 5-6 minutes, until the fish flakes easily. Transfer the steaks to a warmed serving dish.
4 Blend the cornstarch with the water to make a smooth paste and stir into the liquid in the dish. Microwave at 100% (high) for 1-2 minutes, until thick, stirring 2-3 times. Taste and adjust the seasoning if necessary, then pour over the halibut. Garnish with parsley and thyme and serve at once.

TROUT STUFFED WITH SPINACH

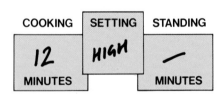

COOKING	SETTING	STANDING
12 MINUTES	HIGH	— MINUTES

¼ lb fresh spinach leaves
½ cup butter
⅔ cup chopped chives
3 slices day-old bread, crusts
   removed and crumbled
salt and black pepper
4 fresh trout, weighing about
   11 oz each cleaned,
   with the tails trimmed
4 Canadian bacon slices
For the garnish:
lemon wedges
chopped chives
fresh coriander sprigs

Serves 4

Peppered Cod Steaks

1 Wash the spinach leaves, strip off their stems, and chop finely.

2 Place the butter in a 1 quart bowl and microwave at 100% (high) for 1-1½ minutes, to melt. Stir in the spinach and chives and microwave at 100% (high) for 2 minutes.

3 Stir in the bread crumbs, and add salt and pepper to taste. Spoon mixture into the trout cavities, pressing edges together.

4 Cover the tails and heads with small strips of smooth foil, checking first that your oven handbook allows this.

5 Place the fish head to tail, in a single layer, in a shallow casserole. Lay a bacon slice on top of each. Cover with a sheet of waxed paper. Microwave at 100% (high) for 4 minutes.

6 Rearrange the trout; re-cover and cook at 100% (high) for 5-6 minutes, or until tender.

7 Arrange on a serving plate, garnish and serve.

PEPPERED COD STEAKS

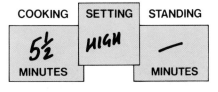

COOKING	SETTING	STANDING
5½ MINUTES	HIGH	— MINUTES

4 frozen cod steaks, weighing about 6 oz each, thawed
2 tablespoons fresh orange or lemon juice
2 tablespoons oil
2-3 tablespoons black peppercorns, crushed, or freshly ground black pepper
4 tomato slices
For the garnish:
1 tablespoon chopped fresh parsley
3 stuffed olives, sliced
watercress sprigs, or blanched broccoli flowerets

Serves 4

1 Put the fish in a shallow dish. Mix the fruit juice with the oil and pour over the fish. Turn the fish over to coat thoroughly, then leave to marinate for 30 minutes, turning once during this time.

2 Remove the cod steaks from the dish with a slotted spoon, reserving the marinade. Coat the fish on both sides with the peppercorns, or season generously with ground pepper, pressing well so the coating sticks to the fish. Return to the dish and cover with pierced plastic wrap.

3 Microwave at 100% (high) for 5-6 minutes or until the fish flakes. Rearrange after 3 minutes. Top the fish with tomato slices and spoon over a little of the marinade. Microwave at 100% (high) for 30 seconds. Place on a serving dish, garnish each cod steak with chopped parsley and stuffed olives and arrange watercress or broccoli in the center of the dish.

FLOUNDER WITH CREAMY MUSTARD SAUCE

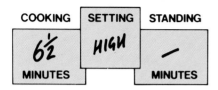

COOKING	SETTING	STANDING
6½ MINUTES	HIGH	— MINUTES

4 large flounder fillets, skinned
6 tablespoons dry white wine
1 tablespoon lemon juice
salt and pepper
¼ cup heavy cream
2 egg yolks
2 teaspoons Dijon mustard
2 teaspoons capers
parsley sprigs, for garnish

Serves 4

1 Roll up the fillets and arrange close together in a shallow dish that will just hold them in a single layer side-by-side. Mix together the wine, lemon juice and salt and pepper to taste. Sprinkle over the fillets.
2 Cover with pierced plastic wrap and microwave at 100% (high) for 5-6 minutes, or until the fish flakes when touched with the point of a knife.
3 Pour the cooking liquid into a 4 cup liquid measure and microwave at 100% (high) for 1 minute, or until boiling. In a small bowl, mix together the cream, egg yolks and mustard. Stir a little of the hot cooking liquid into the cream mix, then stir this mixture into the liquid in the measure, stirring constantly.
4 Microwave at 100% (high) for 30-45 seconds, until the sauce thickens, stirring several times. Do not boil. Stir in the capers, then taste and adjust the seasoning as necessary.
5 Arrange the fish on a warm platter, pour the sauce over and serve at once, garnished with parsley.

Flounder with Creamy Mustard Sauce

RED MULLET WRAP-UPS

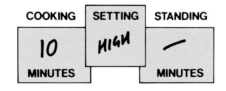

COOKING	SETTING	STANDING
10 MINUTES	HIGH	— MINUTES

4 red mullet, about ½ lb each
2 tablespoons butter
1 tablespoon lemon juice
1-2 tablespoons capers
For the stuffing:
3 tablespoons butter or margarine
1 onion, minced
1½ cups minced mushrooms
½ cup soft wholewheat bread crumbs
2 tablespoons chopped fresh parsley
salt and pepper
For the garnish:
lemon slices
watercress

Serves 4

1 To make the stuffing, put the butter and onion into a bowl and microwave at 100% (high) for 2-3 minutes, until onion is soft. Stir in the mushrooms, the wholewheat breadcrumbs and the chopped parsley. Add salt and pepper to taste and mix.

2 Stuff each mullet with a fourth of the mushroom mixture. Weigh the stuffed fish together and calculate the cooking time at 3-4 minutes per 1 lb total weight.

3 Make 2-3 small diagonal slits in each fish on both sides. Cut a rectangle of waxed paper for each fish, large enough to enclose it, and grease lightly. Spread the center of the paper with butter. Put one fish on each piece of paper and sprinkle with lemon juice.

4 Wrap the head and tail of each mullet in a strip of foil. Check with your manufacturer's handbook to ensure that small pieces of foil may be used for protection. Bring the edges of the paper together to enclose the fish. Fold the edges over once or twice.

5 Arrange the wrapped fish head to tail, on a large plate. Microwave at 100% (high) for half the calculated time. Turn the packages and rearrange. Continue to cook at 100% (high) for the rest of the cooking time.

6 Unwrap the parcels and slide fish onto a hot serving dish. Sprinkle with capers, garnish with lemon and watercress and serve.

Red Mullet Wrap-Ups

CHEESE-TOPPED FISH

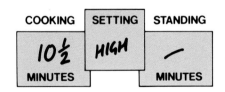

COOKING	SETTING	STANDING
10½ MINUTES	HIGH	╱ MINUTES

1 lb halibut steaks
For the sauce:
2 tablespoons butter or margarine
2 tablespoons all-purpose flour
salt and pepper
pinch of grated nutmeg
1¼ cups milk or half-and-half
For the topping:
1 tablespoon butter or margarine

2 tablespoons soft white bread crumbs
2 tablespoons shredded Cheddar cheese or Monterey Jack
1 teaspoon minced fresh parsley

Serves 2-4

1 Arrange the fish steaks in a ring in a shallow bowl. Cover with pierced plastic wrap and microwave at 100% (high) for 5-6 minutes, turning once. Remove from the microwave oven and set aside, covered, while preparing the sauce.

2 Microwave the butter in a large serving dish at 100% (high) for 30 seconds. Beat in flour, salt and pepper and nutmeg. Beat in milk until well mixed. Microwave at 100% (high) for 3-4 minutes until the sauce is thick and smooth, beating frequently during cooking.

3 Skin fish, then drain and flake, removing any bones. Stir the flaked fish into the sauce.

4 Prepare the topping. Microwave the butter in a small bowl at 100% (high) for 15 seconds. Stir in the remaining ingredients. Sprinkle the topping over the fish and microwave, uncovered, at 100% (high) for 1½-2 minutes or until both the topping and the fish are hot. Serve immediately.

V·E·G·E·T·A·B·L·E D·I·S·H·E·S

Endive in Cheese Sauce

ENDIVE IN CHEESE SAUCE

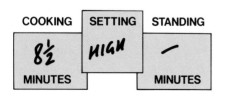

COOKING	SETTING	STANDING
8½ MINUTES	HIGH	— MINUTES

4 heads of Belgian endive
1 teaspoon lemon juice
For the sauce:
2 tablespoons margarine or butter
¼ cup all-purpose flour
1 cup milk
6-8 scallions, very finely sliced
1 package (3 oz) cream cheese
¼ teaspoon Dijon mustard

1½ teaspoons lemon juice
salt and pepper
chopped chives, for garnish

Serves 4

1 Wash the endive heads, trim off any brown edges and cut a thin slice from the bottom of each head. Cut into the endive from the base end to a depth of about 1 inch and twist the knife to remove the hard core.

2 Place the endive in a single layer in a shallow serving dish with ¼ cup water and the juice. Cover with pierced plastic wrap and microwave at 100% (high) for 5-7 minutes, or until tender when pierced with a skewer.

3 To make the sauce, place the margarine in a 3 cup bowl and microwave at 100% (high) for 30 seconds. Sprinkle in the flour and mix. Gradually stir in the milk. Microwave at 100% (high) for 2½-3½ minutes, or until thick and smooth, stirring 2-3 times.

4 Add the scallions to the sauce and microwave at 100% (high) for 40-60 seconds. Beat in the cheese, mustard and lemon juice. Season to taste with salt and pepper. Drain the endive and pour the sauce over. Sprinkle with chopped chives and serve at once.

MIXED VEGETABLES A LA GRECQUE

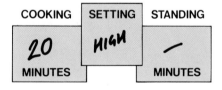

COOKING	SETTING	STANDING
20 MINUTES	HIGH	— MINUTES

2 cups small pearl onions
2 cups frozen green beans
1½ cups thickly sliced button mushrooms
salt and pepper
2 tablespoons chopped fresh parsley
For the sauce:
⅓ cup dry white wine
¼ cup olive oil
¼ cup tomato paste
1 onion, thinly sliced
1 clove garlic, minced
1 teaspoon mustard seed

Serves 4

1 Place the pearl onions in a bowl with ¼ cup water, cover with pierced plastic wrap and microwave at 100% (high) for 5 minutes. Drain thoroughly.

2 To make the sauce, put the wine, olive oil, tomato paste, sliced onion, minced garlic and mustard seed into a 2 quart casserole. Cover the casserole with the lid or with pierced plastic wrap and microwave at 100% (high) for 5 minutes. Stir 2-3 times.

3 Add the pearl onions, beans and mushrooms, re-cover and cook at 100% (high) for 10 minutes, or until the vegetables are tender, stirring halfway through the cooking time. Add salt and pepper to taste.

4 Let the vegetables cool, then transfer to a covered container. Stir in most of the parsley and refrigerate for 30 minutes.

5 Just before serving, remove from the refrigerator and sprinkle with the remaining parsley.

M·I·C·R·O·T·I·P

How well done you like your vegetables is a matter of taste. If you prefer them soft, add more water and cook for a little longer. When warming canned vegetables in the microwave, add a little of the can liquid and cook only for enough time to reheat them.

Mixed Vegetables à la Grecque

BROCCOLI WITH CREAMY CHEESE SAUCE

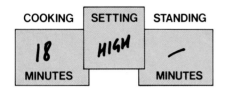

COOKING	SETTING	STANDING
18 MINUTES	HIGH	— MINUTES

2 packages (10 oz each) frozen
   broccoli spears
2 tablespoons margarine or
   butter
¼ cup all-purpose flour
1 cup light cream
1 package (2¾ oz) semisoft
   cheese with garlic and herbs
2 teaspoons minced fresh
   parsley
salt and pepper

Serves 4-6

1 Arrange the broccoli in a rectangular serving dish, with the heads turned toward the center of the dish. Add 2 tablespoons water, cover with pierced plastic wrap and microwave at 100% (high) for 10 minutes.
2 Separate the broccoli, rearrange and re-cover. Microwave at 100% (high) for 5 minutes, drain and rearrange the broccoli in the serving dish, with heads turned toward the outside.
3 Place the margarine in a 3 cup bowl and microwave at 100% (high) for 30 seconds to melt. Stir in the flour, gradually add the cream and mix. Microwave at 100% (high) for 2-3 minutes, or until thick.
4 Cut the cheese in pieces, place in a small bowl and microwave at 100% (high) for 30 seconds, or until well softened. Add to the sauce and stir until melted and smooth.
5 Add the parsley and salt and pepper to taste and pour over the stems of the broccoli, leaving the heads exposed. Serve at once.

Broccoli with Creamy Cheese Sauce

HOT ORANGE BEETS

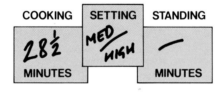

COOKING	SETTING	STANDING
28½ MINUTES	MED/HIGH	— MINUTES

4 cloves
1 onion, cut into
   quarters
1¼ cups milk
2 bay leaves
6 peppercorns
¼ teaspoon ground mace
1 large orange
4 medium uncooked beets
2 tablespoons butter
¼ cup all-purpose flour
¼ teaspoon ground
   cinnamon
salt and white pepper

Serves 4

1 Stick a clove in each onion quarter, then place in a large liquid measure jug with the milk, bay leaves, peppercorns and mace.
2 Remove the rind of the orange with a potato parer, strip the pith away and add half the rind to the milk. Microwave at 50% (medium) for 9-10 minutes, or until boiling. Cover with plastic wrap and let stand for 30 minutes for the flavors to infuse.
3 Prick the beets and place in a 2 quart casserole with ½ cup water and a pinch of salt. Cover with lid and microwave at 100% (high) for 14-16 minutes. Rearrange after 7-8 minutes. The beets are cooked when the skin will rub off easily.
4 Using a sharp knife, cut the remaining orange rind into matchstick strips. Put in a small bowl, add ¼ cup water and microwave at 100% (high) for 3 minutes.

STUFFED LEEKS

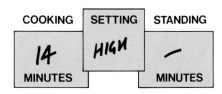

COOKING	SETTING	STANDING
14	*HIGH*	—
MINUTES		MINUTES

8 leeks, trimmed and thoroughly
  washed
salt
½ lb Gorgonzola cheese
1 egg, beaten
1 cup chopped cooked ham
¼ cup butter

Serves 4

1 Place the leeks in a single layer in a dish, add ¼ cup water, cover with pierced plastic wrap and microwave at 100% (high) for 10 minutes. Rearrange after 5 minutes.

2 Meanwhile, using a fork, mash the cheese in a bowl. Add the beaten egg and mix thoroughly together. Stir in the ham.

3 Drain the leeks thoroughly and let stand for about 10 minutes, or until they are cool enough to handle.

4 Using a finger, push out the middle of each leek from the root end to leave a tube. Fill the leeks with the cheese mixture, pressing the mixture in with a teaspoon handle and making sure that the leeks are completely filled all the way through.

5 Return the leeks to the dish, dot with butter and microwave at 100% (high) for 4-5 minutes before serving.

Stuffed Leeks

Drain and rinse with cold water. Drain and reserve. This initial boiling and draining process removes the bitter taste from the orange rind.

5 Squeeze the juice from the orange and reserve. Strain the flavored milk.

6 To make the sauce, place the butter in a 3 cup bowl and microwave at 100% (high) for 30 seconds to melt. Sprinkle in the flour and stir. Gradually stir in the flavored milk, reserved orange juice, cinnamon, and salt and pepper to taste.

7 Microwave at 100% (high) for 1-2 minutes, stirring 2-3 times, until thick and smooth.

8 Drain beets, cut away top and bottom, peel off the skin and slice. Put in a warmed serving dish.

9 Reheat the sauce at 100% (high) for 1 minute, then pour over the beets. Sprinkle with the reserved orange strips and serve.

VEGETABLE TERRINE

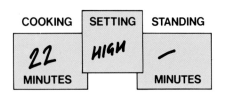

COOKING	SETTING	STANDING
22 MINUTES	HIGH	— MINUTES

12 cabbage leaves, center midribs removed
salt
2/3 cup carrots, cut into matchstick lengths
1 cup zucchini, cut into matchstick lengths
vegetable oil
1 can (7 oz) whole kernel corn with pimiento, drained
2/3 cup milk
3 tablespoons heavy cream
2 eggs
1 egg yolk
1/2 teaspoon grated nutmeg
freshly ground black pepper

For the tomato sauce:
1/2 lb tomatoes, puréed and strained
3 tablespoons plain yogurt
1 teaspoon Dijon mustard
1 teaspoon Worcestershire sauce
1 teaspoon ketchup
pinch of superfine sugar
salt and pepper

Serves 4

1 Place the cabbage leaves in a 2 quart bowl, add 5 cups boiling water and microwave at 100% (high) for 1 minute. Drain the cabbage and dry with a clean dish towel.
2 Place the carrot and zucchini sticks in a 1 quart bowl, add 1/4 cup water, cover with pierced plastic wrap and microwave at 100% (high) for 4 minutes. Drain, rinse under cold water and drain again.
3 Brush an 8½ x 5 inch microwave loaf dish with vegetable oil and line with 3 or 4 of the largest cabbage leaves. Chop all the re-

Vegetable Terrine

maining leaves fairly finely.
4 Put half the carrot and zucchini mixture in the lined loaf dish, add half the corn and pimiento, then half the chopped cabbage. Repeat the layering to make 6 layers in all.
5 Place the milk and cream in a jug and microwave at 100% (high) for 2-2½ minutes until almost boiling.
6 Beat the eggs lightly with the extra yolk and the nutmeg. Season with salt and pepper and add the milk and cream. Carefully pour the egg mixture into the loaf dish, gently easing the vegetables apart in several places with a slim spatula, to make sure the egg mixture is evenly distributed through the terrine and goes right to the base of the dish. Fold any protruding cabbage leaves over the filling and cover the dish

with pierced plastic wrap.
7 Set the loaf dish in a larger dish. Pour in hot water to come halfway up the side of the loaf dish and microwave at 100% (high) for 15 minutes until the custard is set and firm to the touch. Remove the loaf dish from the water and let cool. Chill overnight in the refrigerator.
8 To make the sauce, mix the strained tomato paste with the remaining sauce ingredients, stirring to make sure they are well combined. Season to taste. Cover with plastic wrap and chill for at least 2 hours.
9 To serve, let the terrine stand at room temperature for about 10 minutes. Run a knife around the side of the terrine and invert on a serving platter, shaking gently to unmold. Serve cut in slices with the tomato sauce.

VEGETABLES IN CURRY SAUCE

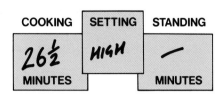

COOKING	SETTING	STANDING
26½ MINUTES	HIGH	— MINUTES

2 cups frozen cauliflower
  flowerets
1¼ cups frozen sliced carrots
1 package (10 oz) frozen green
  beans
1 package (10 oz) frozen lima
  beans
salt
For the sauce:
3 tablespoons margarine
6 tablespoons plain flour
1 tablespoon mild curry
  powder
¼ teaspoon ground ginger
1¼ cups hot vegetable stock
2 tablespoons fresh orange
  juice
1 cup milk
pepper
2 tablespoons light cream or
  half-and-half
Accompaniments:
¼ cup split almonds
1 cup raw long-grain rice,
  cooked
sprig of mint
Serves 4

1 Place all the vegetables in a 2 quart casserole with ¼ cup water. Cover and microwave at 100% (high) for 18 minutes, stirring twice. Drain and add salt.
2 To make the sauce, place the margarine in a 1 quart bowl and microwave at 100% (high) for 30-45 seconds to melt. Add the flour and stir to form a smooth paste. Stir in the curry powder and ginger.
3 Microwave at 100% (high) for 1 minute. Gradually pour on the stock, orange juice and milk, stirring continuously. Microwave at 100% (high) for 3-4 minutes, stirring 2-3 times. Add pepper to taste and mix in the cream or half-and-half, stirring well to blend with the curry mixture.
4 Pour the sauce over the vegetables, lightly tossing them with a fork to coat.
5 Place the almonds on a plate and microwave at 100% (high) for 4-5 minutes, stirring 2-3 times.
6 Arrange the vegetables on a serving dish on top of a bed of rice. Garnish with the sprig of mint and sprinkle with browned almonds.

ASPARAGUS VINAIGRETTE

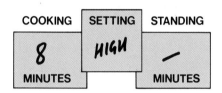

COOKING	SETTING	STANDING
8 MINUTES	HIGH	— MINUTES

1 lb fresh asparagus stalks,
  trimmed
For the sauce:
½ cup olive oil
2 tablespoons lemon juice
2 tablespoons tarragon vinegar
2 teaspoons chopped fresh
  herbs (optional)
salt and pepper

Serves 4

1 Place the asparagus in a rectangular, shallow dish. Arrange with the thick stalks to the outside of the dish and the tender tips toward the center.
2 Add 6 tablespoons water, and cover with pierced plastic wrap. Microwave at 100% (high) for 8-10 minutes, or until tender, giving a half turn after 5 minutes.
3 Drain and place the asparagus on a serving platter.
4 To make the sauce, beat the oil in a bowl and gradually add the remaining ingredients, beating continuously until thoroughly blended.
5 Pour the sauce over the asparagus, or pass separately in a sauceboat.

Vegetables in Curry Sauce

LIMA BEANS & PARSLEY SAUCE

COOKING	SETTING	STANDING
12½ MINUTES	HIGH	— MINUTES

1½ packages (10 oz each)
   frozen lima beans
sprig of fresh rosemary or pinch
   of dried rosemary
For the sauce:
2 tablespoons margarine or
   butter
3 tablespoons all-purpose flour
⅔ cup milk
⅔ cup hot vegetable stock
¼ cup finely chopped fresh
   parsley
salt and pepper

Serves 4

1 Put the beans, rosemary and 2 tablespoons water in a 2 quart serving dish. Cover with pierced plastic wrap and microwave at 100% (high) for 9-10 minutes.
2 Drain the beans and discard the sprig of rosemary, if used. Cover the beans and set aside.
3 To make the sauce, place the margarine in a 1 quart bowl and microwave at 100% (high) for 30 seconds to melt. Sprinkle in the flour and stir, then add the milk and hot stock. Microwave at 100% (high) for 2-3 minutes until thickened, stirring 2 or 3 times.
4 Stir in half the parsley and salt and pepper to taste and work in a blender or food processor until smooth. Return to the rinsed-out bowl, add the remaining parsley and microwave at 100% (high) for 1 minute.
5 Pour the sauce over the lima beans and serve.

MASHED MEDLEY

COOKING	SETTING	STANDING
13 MINUTES	HIGH	— MINUTES

¾ lb parsnips, cut in 1 inch cubes
½ lb rutabagas, cut in 1 inch
   cubes
½ lb carrots, cut in 1 inch slices
3 tablespoons margarine or
   butter
3 tablespoons milk or light cream
salt and pepper
For the garnish:
pinch of paprika
pinch of ground coriander
pinch of grated nutmeg
sprig of parsley

Serves 4

Lima Beans & Parsley Sauce

1 Place vegetables in 3 small bowls, keeping the varieties separate. Add ¼ cup water to each.

2 Cover with pierced plastic wrap and microwave all three together on 100% (high) for 13-15 minutes. Check after 12 minutes to see if any vegetables are cooked. Remove the bowls as each variety is cooked.

3 Add 1 tablespoon margarine and 1 tablespoon milk or cream to each dish and mash. Add salt and pepper to taste.

4 Arrange in sections on a circular dish. To garnish, sprinkle paprika on the parsnips, coriander on the carrots and nutmeg on the rutabagas. Finish with a sprig of parsley and serve.

Mashed Medley

COUNTRY-STYLE BRUSSELS SPROUTS

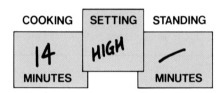

COOKING	SETTING	STANDING
14 MINUTES	HIGH	— MINUTES

2 packages (10 oz each) frozen Brussels sprouts
1 tablespoon vegetable oil
1 large onion, sliced
1 green pepper, seeded and chopped
1 lb tomatoes, peeled and roughly chopped
½ teaspoon dried basil
salt and pepper

Serves 4

1 Place the sprouts in a 2 quart serving dish, add ¼ cup water and cover with pierced plastic wrap. Microwave at 100% (high) for 9-11 minutes, stirring 2-3 times. Drain thoroughly.

2 Place the oil, onion and green pepper in a 1 quart bowl and microwave at 100% (high) for 3-4 minutes, stirring 2-3 times.

3 Add the tomatoes and basil, stir and microwave at 100% (high) for 2 minutes. Add salt and pepper to taste and mix well into the sprouts. Serve at once.

FARMHOUSE LENTILS

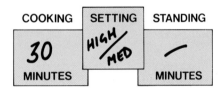

COOKING	SETTING	STANDING
30 MINUTES	HIGH/MED	— MINUTES

1 tablespoon vegetable oil
1 large onion, thinly sliced
4 cups hot vegetable stock
4 potatoes, (about 1 lb) cut in even-sized chunks
1 ¼ cups split red lentils
½ teaspoon dried marjoram or thyme
½ teaspoon paprika
salt and pepper
4 tomatoes, peeled, quartered and seeded
⅔ cup frozen peas
1 cup thinly sliced button mushrooms

Serves 4

1 Place the oil in a 3 quart casserole, add the onion and microwave at 100% (high) for 2 minutes.

2 Add the hot stock and microwave at 100% (high) for 3 minutes, or until boiling. Add the potatoes, lentils, herbs, paprika and salt and pepper to taste. Stir well, then cover with pierced plastic wrap and microwave at 100% (high) for 15 minutes, stirring occasionally.

3 Add the tomatoes, peas and mushrooms, re-cover and microwave at 50% (medium) for 10 minutes. Stir well.

4 Before serving, taste and adjust the seasoning, if necessary, then transfer to a warmed shallow dish. Serve hot.

M·I·C·R·O·T·I·P

A microwave oven is ideal for cooking frozen French fries or hash browns. Preheat a browning dish for 5 minutes, add 2 tablespoons oil and ½ lb frozen hash browns and microwave at 100% (high) for 7 minutes, stirring midway through the cooking time.

CREAMED LEMON SPINACH

COOKING	SETTING	STANDING
11 MINUTES	HIGH	— MINUTES

2 packages (10 oz each) frozen
   leaf spinach
2 tablespoons margarine or
   butter
2 tablespoons all-purpose flour
2/3 cup heavy cream
grated rind and juice of 1/2 lemon
salt and pepper
pinch of grated nutmeg
For the garnish:
2 hard-cooked eggs, yolks and
   whites separated and finely
   chopped
lemon slices

Serves 4

1 Place the spinach in a rectangular dish. Cover with pierced plastic wrap and microwave at 100% (high) for 8-10 minutes, stirring twice.
2 Turn the cooked spinach into a strainer and drain thoroughly. Press with the back of a large spoon to extract all the moisture.
3 Place the margarine in a 2 quart bowl and microwave at 100% (high) for 30 seconds to melt. Sprinkle in the flour and stir. Gradually add the cream and mix thoroughly.
4 Microwave at 100% (high) for 1 1/2-2 minutes, stirring twice. Add lemon rind and juice, and salt, pepper and nutmeg to taste.
5 Stir the spinach into the cream sauce and microwave at 100% (high) for 1 minute.
6 Turn into a heated serving dish and arrange the chopped hard-cooked eggs in rows over the top. Before serving, garnish with quartered lemon slices.

Creamed Lemon Spinach

RICE MOLD

COOKING	SETTING	STANDING
15 MINUTES	HIGH	— MINUTES

2/3 cup long-grain rice
salt
1 tablespoon vegetable oil
4 tablespoons frozen whole
   kernel corn
1 jar (6 oz) pimientos,
   drained
1 green pepper, seeded and
   chopped
2 tomatoes, peeled,
   seeded and chopped
2 scallions, thinly sliced
2 tablespoons almonds, chopped
1 tablespoon seedless raisins
1 tablespoon golden raisins
watercress sprigs, for garnish
For the dressing:
1/3 cup olive oil
1 tablespoon red wine vinegar
2 teaspoons lemon juice
1 teaspoon superfine sugar
1 teaspoon mild curry powder
salt

Serves 4-6

1 Place the rice in a large deep bowl and add 2 cups boiling salted water and the vegetable oil. Cover with pierced plastic wrap and microwave at 100% (high) for 12 minutes.
2 Drain the rice in a strainer, rinse under cold running water, drain again and turn into a large bowl.
3 Place the corn in a small bowl with 2 tablespoons water. Cover with pierced plastic wrap and microwave at 100% (high) for 3 minutes. Let cool.
4 Chop one of the canned pimientos and cut the remainder in long thin strips, about 1/2 inch wide. Reserve the strips for garnish.
5 Stir the chopped pimiento into the rice together with the green pepper, tomatoes, scallions, almonds, corn, raisins and golden raisins. Mix well so that the vegetables are well distributed.
6 To make the dressing, place all the ingredients in a screw-top jar. Season with salt and shake well. Mix into the rice.
7 Pack the rice mixture into a 3 cup gelatin mold, pushing it firmly down with the back of a large spoon. Cover the bowl with

plastic wrap and chill for at least 2 hours.

8 Unmold the rice salad onto a platter. Arrange pimiento on the top in a wheel pattern and garnish with watercress.

MIXED BEAN CASSEROLE

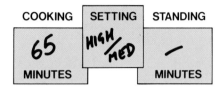

COOKING	SETTING	STANDING
65 MINUTES	HIGH/MED	— MINUTES

½ cup navy beans
½ cup adzuki or kidney beans
½ cup black-eyed peas
1 green pepper, seeded
2 tablespoons vegetable oil
1 large onion, chopped
1 small head celery, chopped
2 cloves garlic, crushed
1 can (1 lb 13 oz) tomatoes
2 cups hot vegetable stock
2 teaspoons dried oregano
salt and pepper

Serves 4-6

1 Put all the beans in a large bowl, cover with water and let soak overnight.

2 Drain the beans, rinse under running water, drain and put into a 3 quart bowl with 5 cups cold water. Cover with pierced plastic wrap and microwave at 100% (high) for 20 minutes.

3 Meanwhile, cut a few slices from green pepper and reserve for garnish. Finely chop the remainder and place in a 2 quart bowl with the oil, onion, celery and garlic, if using. Microwave at 100% (high) for 5 minutes, stirring 2-3 times.

4 Add the tomatoes with their juice, the hot stock, oregano and salt and pepper to taste. Cover and microwave at 100% (high) for 5 minutes.

5 Drain the beans, add the vegetable mixture, cover with pierced plastic wrap and microwave at 50% (medium) for 35-45 minutes, or until the beans are tender.

6 Adjust the seasoning, if necessary. Transfer to a warmed serving dish, garnish with green pepper and serve at once.

LEEK & TOMATO CASSEROLE

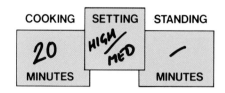

COOKING	SETTING	STANDING
20 MINUTES	HIGH/MED	— MINUTES

2 large leeks, trimmed, washed and cut in 1 inch pieces
2 large onions, cut in 8 pieces
1 can (16 oz) tomatoes
1 tablespoon chopped fresh parsley
1 bay leaf
2 cloves garlic, crushed
1 teaspoon salt
pepper
⅔ cup hot chicken or vegetable stock
1 tablespoon vegetable oil
1 tablespoon lemon juice
pinch of dried thyme
chopped fresh parsley, for garnish

Serves 4-6

1 Mix all the ingredients, except the garnish, in a 2 quart casserole.
2 Cover with pierced plastic wrap and microwave at 100% (high) for 10 minutes, stirring 2-3 times.
3 Reduce the power to 50% (medium) and microwave for a further 10 minutes, or until tender. Stir, remove the bay leaf and serve sprinkled with parsley.

Rice Mold

M·I·C·R·O·T·I·P

To save time, use frozen rice (long-grain, brown or saffron) in a recipe or to serve with another dish. It is partially cooked and needs a very short time in a microwave oven. Place in a bowl, cover with pierced plastic wrap and microwave at 100% (high) for 4 minutes per ½-¾ lb.

STIR-FRIED BEANS & BEAN SPROUTS

COOKING	SETTING	STANDING
5 MINUTES	HIGH	— MINUTES

2 tablespoons vegetable oil
1 onion, sliced
½ lb small green beans, left whole
1 tablespoon soy sauce
1 tablespoon lemon juice
pepper
½ cup small button mushrooms
4 cups bean sprouts

Serves 4

1 Preheat a large browning dish at 100% (high) for 5 minutes, or according to manufacturer's directions.
2 Add the vegetable oil, onion and beans, stir and cover with the lid. Microwave at 100% (high) for 3 minutes.
3 Add 2 tablespoons water, the soy sauce and lemon juice, together with pepper to taste. Add the mushrooms and the bean sprouts and mix together. Microwave, uncovered, at 100% (high) for 2-3 minutes, until vegetables are heated through but still crisp.
4 Transfer to a warmed serving dish and serve immediately.

SWEET & SOUR CARROTS

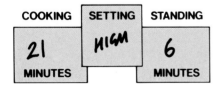

COOKING	SETTING	STANDING
21 MINUTES	HIGH	6 MINUTES

3 cups thickly sliced carrots
2 tablespoons vegetable oil
1 onion, sliced
3 celery stalks, sliced

Stir-Fried Beans & Bean Sprouts

salt and pepper
¼ cup halved blanched almonds
For the sauce:
2 teaspoons cornstarch
2 teaspoons soy sauce

1 tablespoon light brown sugar
1 tablespoon cider vinegar
2 teaspoons lemon juice
⅔ cup hot vegetable stock

Serves 4

72

Mushrooms & Garlic Peas

2 Cream the butter and mix in the chopped mushroom stems, garlic, parsley, salt and pepper.
3 Spoon the peas onto the mushroom caps. Dot with the butter.
4 Cover with waxed paper and microwave at 100% (high) for 2-3 minutes, until heated, rotating the plate once or twice.
5 Place on a serving platter and serve immediately.

SPICY VEGETABLES

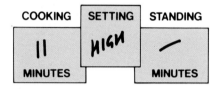

COOKING	SETTING	STANDING
11 MINUTES	HIGH	— MINUTES

1 tablespoon oil
¼ cup margarine or butter
2 cloves garlic, crushed
1 tablespoon ground coriander
2 teaspoons ground cumin
3 tablespoons hot vegetable stock
1 package (10 oz) frozen lima beans
3 cups sliced leeks
2 cups even-sized broccoli flowerets
1 large sweet red pepper, seeded and cut in thin strips
pepper
1 teaspoon lemon juice

Serves 4-6

1 Put the oil, margarine, garlic, coriander and cumin in a 2 quart casserole. Cover with a lid and microwave at 100% (high) for 2 minutes, stirring after 1 minute.
2 Stir in the stock. Add the lima beans, leeks and broccoli, re-cover and microwave at 100% (high) for 5 minutes. Add the red pepper, re-cover and microwave at 100% (high) for 4-5 minutes, or until vegetables are tender-crisp. Stir after 3 minutes.
3 Season with pepper, add the lemon juice, stir and serve.

1 Place the carrots in a 2 quart bowl with ½ cup cold water. Cover with pierced plastic wrap and microwave at 100% (high) for 10-12 minutes. Stir midway through the cooking time. Let stand.
2 Place the oil, sliced onion and celery stalks in a 2 quart casserole and microwave at 100% (high) for 4 minutes, stirring after 2 minutes.
3 Mix in the cornstarch, then add the soy sauce, brown sugar, vinegar, lemon juice and stock and stir to blend the ingredients. Microwave at 100% (high) for 2-3 minutes, until boiling, stirring 2-3 times.
4 Add the carrots, cover with pierced plastic wrap and microwave at 100% (high) for 5 minutes. Add plenty of salt and pepper. Scatter the halved blanched almonds over the surface and serve immediately.

MUSHROOMS & GARLIC PEAS

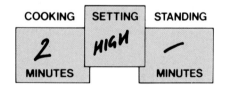

COOKING	SETTING	STANDING
2 MINUTES	HIGH	— MINUTES

8 medium mushrooms
¼ cup butter or margarine
2 cloves garlic, crushed
2 tablespoons chopped fresh parsley
salt and pepper
1 cup frozen peas

Serves 4

1 Remove the mushroom stems from the caps and chop them finely. Wipe the mushroom caps and place them, gill sides up, around the edge of a plate lined with paper towels.

Lemon-Studded Artichokes

BEAN-STUFFED POTATOES

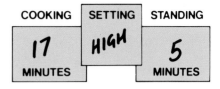

COOKING	SETTING	STANDING
17 MINUTES	HIGH	5 MINUTES

4 potatoes(about ½ lb each), scrubbed
salt and pepper
1 can (5 oz) baked beans
¾ cup shredded sharp Cheddar cheese or Monterey Jack

Serves 4

1 Prick each potato with a fork. Wrap in paper towels. Put in oven at least 1 inch apart. Microwave at 100% (high) for 15 minutes, turning over and rearranging after 8 minutes.
2 Wrap the potatoes in foil when just tender and let stand for 5 minutes, or until they feel soft.
3 Unwrap and discard foil. Cut a cross in the top of each potato and squeeze at the bottom so the cross opens up. Add salt and pepper and place the potatoes on a plate.
4 Place a spoonful of beans in each cavity, and sprinkle with cheese. Microwave at 100% (high) for 2-3 minutes to heat the filling and melt the cheese, rearranging midway through the cooking time. Serve the potatoes immediately.

M·I·C·R·O·T·I·P

Baked potatoes take only minutes to cook in a microwave, but it is important to prick them all over with a fork first otherwise they will burst. Turn them over half way through cooking to avoid hard patches developing on the bases.

LEMON-STUDDED ARTICHOKES

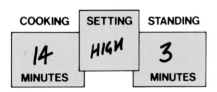

COOKING	SETTING	STANDING
14 MINUTES	HIGH	3 MINUTES

8 thin lemon slices
4 whole, fresh artichokes, trimmed, rinsed and drained
1 cup butter

Serves 4

1 Cut 2 lemon slices into 8 wedges and tuck into the outer leaves of 1 artichoke with the lemon peel showing. Repeat with the remaining lemon slices and artichokes.
2 Wrap each artichoke in plastic wrap, arrange in a ring on a plate and microwave at 100% (high) for 12-15 minutes or until the lower leaves can be easily pulled off. Rotate and rearrange once. Let stand for 3-5 minutes.
3 Meanwhile, microwave the butter in a covered bowl at 100% (high) for 2-2½ minutes, or until melted. Unwrap the artichokes, remove the chokes and arrange the artichokes on a serving platter. Pour a little of the melted butter into the center of each artichoke and pass the remaining butter separately in a small serving jug.

CHEESY PEAS & ONIONS

COOKING.	SETTING	STANDING
5 MINUTES	HIGH	3 MINUTES

1 package (10 oz) frozen peas
¼ lb pearl onions, peeled
1 tablespoon water
1 tablespoon butter or margarine
½ teaspoon dried chervil or marjoram
salt and pepper
1 tablespoon grated Parmesan cheese, for garnish

Serves 4

1 In a 3 quart casserole, combine the peas, onions and water. cover with pierced plastic wrap.
2 Microwave at 100% (high) for 5-6 minutes, or until the vegetables are tender, stirring once during the cooking time.
3 Stir in the butter, chervil, salt and pepper. Let stand, covered, for 3-5 minutes. Sprinkle with the cheese and serve immediately.

Cheesy Peas & Onions

CHAPTER SEVEN

D·E·S·S·E·R·T·S

Pineapple Mallow

PINEAPPLE MALLOW

COOKING	SETTING	STANDING
3 MINUTES	HIGH	⁄ MINUTES

½ cup butter, cut in pieces
32 Graham cracker squares, finely crushed
For the filling:
26 large marshmallows (about ½ lb)
½ cup medium dry white wine
1 can (16 oz) crushed pineapple, drained, with half the juice reserved

2 teaspoons unflavored gelatin
water
1¼ cups heavy cream
To decorate:
mint sprigs
lightly beaten egg white
superfine sugar
pineapple rings

Serves 8

MICROTIP

To achieve the greatest volume, bring chilled egg whites to room temperature before beating. Microwave them at 100% (high) for 5-10 seconds per egg, then beat immediately with a pinch of salt.

1 Very lightly grease a 9 inch springform pan.

2 Place the butter pieces in a small bowl and microwave at 100% (high) for 1-2 minutes to melt. Mix into the cracker crumbs, then press evenly over the base of the pan. Refrigerate.

3 To make the filling, place the marshmallows and wine in a 2 quart bowl and microwave at 100% (high) for 2-3 minutes. Stir 2-3 times to dissolve the marshmallows. Stir in the reserved pineapple juice.

4 Sprinkle the gelatin over ¼ cup water in a small bowl. Let soak for 5 minutes. Microwave at 100% (high) for 15-30 seconds to dissolve. Do not boil.

5 Stir the gelatin into the marshmallow mixture, then leave for about 30 minutes, until thick but not set.

6 Beat the cream to soft peaks, then fold it into the mixture. Cover and refrigerate for about 15 minutes, until almost set.

7 Pour half the mixture into the prepared pan and carefully spoon the crushed pineapple mixture on top. Spread the remaining mixture over the pineapple. Cover and refrigerate for at least 8 hours, until set.

8 For the decoration, brush sprigs of mint with egg white, then dip in superfine sugar. Dry on a wire rack.

9 Remove the side of the pan and decorate the dessert with halved pineapple rings and mint. Serve chilled.

Honeyed Apricot Whips

HONEYED APRICOT WHIPS

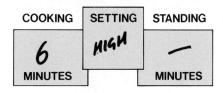

COOKING	SETTING	STANDING
6 MINUTES	HIGH	— MINUTES

1 cup dried apricots
1¼ cups hot water
2 tablespoons honey
1¼ cups plain
   yogurt
2 egg whites
Accompaniments
*ladyfingers or vanilla
   wafers or other cookies*

Serves 4

1 Put the apricots in a 1½ quart bowl with the hot water and honey. Cover with pierced plastic wrap and microwave at 100% (high) for 6-7 minutes, or until the apricots are tender. Let cool completely.

2 Purée the apricots with the cooking syrup and yogurt in a blender or food processor. Alternatively, press the apricots through a strainer, then stir in the cooking syrup and fold in the yogurt.

3 Beat the egg whites to soft peaks. Using a metal spoon, lightly stir 1 tablespoon of the beaten egg white into the apricot mixture then fold in remainder.

4 Spoon the whip into glasses and serve with the ladyfingers.

STRAWBERRY CHARLOTTE RUSSE

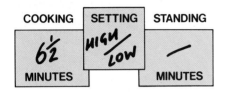

COOKING	SETTING	STANDING
6½ MINUTES	HIGH/LOW	— MINUTES

*1 package (3 oz) strawberry-
  flavored gelatin*
about 25 ladyfingers
1 envelope unflavored gelatin
1¼ cups milk
3 egg yolks
2 tablespoons superfine sugar
2-3 drops vanilla
1¼ cups heavy cream, whipped
*⅓ pint fresh strawberries,
  hulled and sliced*

To decorate:
a few fresh strawberries, halved
½ cup heavy cream, whipped

Serves 6

1 Rinse the base of an 8 inch charlotte russe mold with water, pouring off the excess. Brush the inside of the rim lightly with oil.

2 Place the gelatin in a 2 cup liquid measure. Add ⅔ cup hot water and microwave at 100% (high) for 15-30 seconds to melt. Stir well and make up to 1¼ cups with cold water. Pour into the base of the mold and refrigerate for about 15 minutes to set.

3 Line the side of the mold with the ladyfingers, tapering the ends at the base of the mold if necessary.

4 Sprinkle the unflavored gelatin over 3 tablespoons cold water in a small bowl. Let soak for 5 minutes or until required.

5 Place the milk in a deep measuring cup and microwave at 100% (high) for 3 minutes, or until almost boiling.

6 Cream the egg yolks, sugar and vanilla together until light and creamy. Stir in the milk. Microwave at 100% (high) for 1 minute, then at 30% (low) for 1-2 minutes, or until the custard thickens and will coat the back of a wooden spoon. Beat several times during cooking. Do not boil.

7 Strain the custard into a bowl. Microwave the gelatin at 100% (high) for 15-30 seconds to dissolve. Do not boil. Stir into the custard.

8 Divide the custard and gelatin mixture in half. Place one half in a bowl, set in a larger bowl of ice and let stand until cool. When almost setting, mix in half the whipped cream. Pour into the charlotte mold. Refrigerate for 10 minutes, or until the mixture is set. Arrange the sliced strawberries on top.

9 Cool the remaining custard in the same way, add the cream and pour on top of the strawberries. Refrigerate until set.

10 With a sharp knife, trim the ladyfingers level with the filling. Dip the bottom of the mold in a bowl of hot water for 1-2 seconds, then invert it on a serving platter.

11 Decorate with sliced strawberries and whipped cream before serving.

Strawberry Charlotte Russe

ENGLISH SUMMER PUDDING

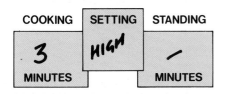

COOKING	SETTING	STANDING
3 MINUTES	HIGH	— MINUTES

¾ pint mixed black and red currants, without stems
½ cup superfine sugar
1 tablespoon orange juice or water
¾ pint raspberries
5-7 thin slices day-old white bread, crusts removed

Serves 4

1 Put the currants into a 2 quart bowl. Add the superfine sugar and orange juice or water, cover with pierced plastic wrap and microwave at 100% (high) for 2-3 minutes, or until the currants are soft and the juices flowing.
2 Add the raspberries, re-cover and microwave at 100% (high) for 1-2 minutes. Let cool.
3 Meanwhile, use most of the bread to line the base and side of a 3 cup pudding mold. Cut the bread so that it fits neatly and use the trimmings to fill any gaps.
4 Put ⅓ cup of the fruit juices and 2 tablespoons of fruit into separate small containers, cover and reserve in the refrigerator. Spoon the remaining fruits and juices into the mold and cover completely with remaining bread.
5 Put a small plate or lid which fits just inside the rim of the mold on top of the pudding. Weight the plate down, then refrigerate the pudding overnight.
6 To serve, run a slim spatula around the top edge of the pudding to loosen it, then invert it on a serving platter. Spoon the reserved fruit juices over any areas of bread that are not colored by the fruit juices and top the pudding with reserved fruit.

Chilled Cassis Soufflé

CHILLED CASSIS SOUFFLE

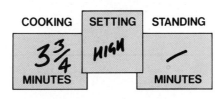

COOKING	SETTING	STANDING
3¾ MINUTES	HIGH	— MINUTES

2 teaspoons unflavored gelatin
4 large eggs, separated
2 tablespoons superfine sugar
7 tablespoons Crème de Cassis
3 tablespoons lemon juice
1 tablespoon black currant jelly
⅔ cup heavy cream
whipped cream, to decorate
For the black currant sauce:
4 tablespoons black currant jelly
¼ cup superfine sugar
2 tablespoons lemon juice

Serves 4-6

1 Prepare a 3 cup soufflé mold by tying a 2 inch collar of non-stick parchment around the mold so that it stands 1 inch above the rim.
2 Sprinkle the gelatin over 2 tablespoons water in a cup and let stand until soft.

3 Meanwhile, place the egg yolks, sugar, Crème de Cassis and lemon juice in a large bowl and mix. Microwave at 100% (high) for 30 seconds. Beat with electric beaters until thick and foamy.
4 Microwave the gelatin at 100% (high) for 15-30 seconds to melt. Do not boil. Stir in the jelly and microwave at 100% (high) for 1 minute until the jelly dissolves. Stir into the lemon mixture. Whip the cream to soft peaks and fold in.
5 Partially fill a bowl with ice cubes. Stand the bowl containing the soufflé mixture on top and stir until it begins to set.
6 Beat the egg whites to soft peaks. Fold into the soufflé mixture with a large metal spoon. Pour into the prepared soufflé mold and chill to set.
7 Meanwhile, to make the sauce, put the jelly, sugar and 1¼ cups water in a 1 quart bowl. Microwave for 2-3 minutes, stirring 2-3 times. Add the lemon juice, stir thoroughly and cool.
8 Remove the collar from the soufflé. Pipe whipped cream around the top edge and serve with the chilled sauce.

CHOCOLATE NUTTY TAPIOCA

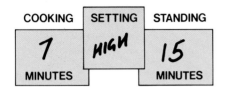

COOKING	SETTING	STANDING
7	**HIGH**	**15**
MINUTES		MINUTES

3 tablespoons quick-cooking
   tapioca
2½ cups milk
2 tablespoons light brown sugar
For the topping:
¼ cup chopped cashews
1 square (1 oz) semisweet
   chocolate, grated

Serves 4

1 Put the tapioca in a 2 quart bowl, add the milk, stir and microwave at 100% (high) for 5-6 minutes, or until boiling. Stir 2-3 times.
2 Stir in sugar. Microwave at 100% (high) for 1 minute. Let stand for 15 minutes, stirring the mixture once during the standing time.
3 Preheat the broiler to moderate. Turn the tapioca into a shallow heatproof dish, level the surface and sprinkle with the chopped cashew nuts and the grated chocolate.
4 Broil for 1-2 minutes, until the chocolate melts and the nuts brown. Serve the tapioca either hot or cold.

LEMON CREAM PIE

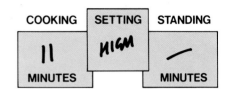

COOKING	SETTING	STANDING
11	**HIGH**	**—**
MINUTES		MINUTES

½ cup butter
2 tablespoons light corn
   syrup
33 Graham cracker squares,
   finely crushed
For the filling:
4 lemons
⅔ cup cornstarch
¾ cup granulated sugar
4 large egg yolks

Chocolate Nutty Tapioca

For the topping:
1 ¼ cups heavy cream
1 tablespoon superfine sugar
yellow nonpareils
angelica

Serves 6-8

1 Place the butter and syrup in a 1 quart bowl and microwave at 100% (high) for 1-1½ minutes, stirring 2-3 times.
2 Add the cracker crumbs and mix. Place a 10 inch pie ring on a flat serving platter. Spoon in the crumb crust mixture and press it evenly over the base and up the side. Refrigerate.
3 To make the filling, thinly pare the rind from the lemons. Place in a bowl with 2½ cups water. Microwave at 100% (high) for 5 minutes. Cover and let stand for 10 minutes. Discard the rind.
4 Squeeze and strain the lemon juice from the lemons. Mix the cornstarch with a little cold water until smooth. Add the juice and cornstarch to the reserved lemon water and mix. Microwave at 100% (high) for 5-6 minutes, stirring 3-4 times, until thick. Stir in the sugar and beat in the egg yolks.
5 Strain into the crumb crust and smooth the top. Refrigerate for 3-4 hours to set.
6 Carefully remove the pie ring from the pie. To make the topping, whip the cream with the sugar to soft peaks, then spoon into a pastry bag fitted with a star tip. Pipe cream on top of the filling, then decorate with yellow decors and angelica. Serve the pie chilled.

Orange & Date Suet Pudding

ORANGE & DATE SUET PUDDING

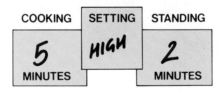

COOKING	SETTING	STANDING
5 MINUTES	*HIGH*	**2** MINUTES

6 tablespoons light syrup
4 thin slices unpeeled fresh orange, seeds removed
¾ cup self-rising flour
1½ cups soft white bread crumbs
6 tablespoons shredded beef suet
¼ cup sugar
⅓ cup chopped dates
1 egg, lightly beaten
⅓ cup milk

Serves 4-6

1 Lightly grease a 4 cup pudding mold. Spoon the syrup into the base of the mold. Place 1 of the orange slices in the base. Cut the remaining 3 slices in quarters, and arrange, overlapping, around the edge of the base on top of the syrup.
2 Sift the flour into a bowl, then stir in the bread crumbs, suet, sugar and dates. Stir in the egg and milk to give a soft dropping consistency.
3 Spoon the suet mixture carefully into the prepared mold and level the surface. Cover with pierced plastic wrap.
4 Microwave at 100% (high) for 5-6 minutes, or until well risen. Remove the plastic wrap carefully and let stand for 2-3 minutes. Invert the pudding onto a warmed serving dish and serve immediately.

M·I·C·R·O·T·I·P

To get more juice, warm oranges and lemons before squeezing. Microwave 1-2 fruits at 100% (high) for 30-45 seconds.

APRICOT & CHERRY COMPOTE

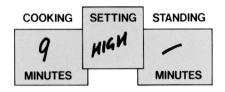

COOKING	SETTING	STANDING
9 MINUTES	HIGH	**—** MINUTES

½ lb dried apricots
finely grated rind and juice of 2
    large oranges
2 inch piece cinnamon
    stick
4 teaspoons honey
1 tablespoon arrowroot
1 cup red wine
1 can (16 oz) pitted Bing
    cherries, drained with
    ⅔ cup cherry syrup
    reserved
¼ teaspoon grated nutmeg

Serves 4

1 Put the apricots in a bowl with the orange rind and juice, cinnamon stick and honey. Mix together, then cover with pierced plastic wrap and set aside.
2 Blend the arrowroot with a little of the wine, then slowly stir in the rest of the wine and the cherry syrup. Stir in the nutmeg.
3 Microwave at 100% (high) for 4-5 minutes until clear and slightly thickened, stirring 2-3 times. Add the cherries and microwave at 100% (high) for a further 2 minutes. Let cool.
4 Microwave the apricots at 100% (high) for 3 minutes, stir and let cool.
5 Just before serving, discard the cinnamon stick. Drain the fruits, reserving the syrups. Spoon the apricots into the center of a serving dish and surround with the cherries. Or simply mix the two fruits together.
6 Mix the drained syrups together and spoon over the fruit.

Apricot & Cherry Compote

HOT BANANA CRUMBLE

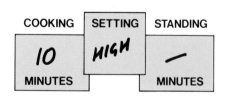

COOKING	SETTING	STANDING
10 MINUTES	HIGH	**—** MINUTES

2 tablespoons cornstarch
2 tablespoons sugar
2½ cups milk
grated rind of ½ lemon
4 firm bananas
1½ teaspoons lemon
    juice

Hot Banana Crumble

For the topping:
1 cup all-purpose flour
¼ cup margarine or butter, diced
2 tablespoons sugar
2 tablespoons slivered almonds
2 tablespoons light brown sugar

Serves 4-6

1 Stir the cornstarch with the sugar and 1 tablespoon milk in a small bowl until smooth. Mix in the remaining milk. Microwave at 100% (high) for 3-4 minutes or until thick, stirring 2-3 times. Stir in the lemon rind.
2 Slice the bananas into a 7 cup pie dish and sprinkle them with the lemon juice. Pour in the prepared dessert mixture, mix thoroughly, then level the surface.
3 Sift the flour into a wide bowl. Add the margarine and cut it in, then stir in the sugar.
4 Sprinkle the topping over the banana dessert, covering the surface completely. Scatter the slivered almonds and the brown sugar over the top. Return the dish to the oven and microwave at 100% (high) for 7-8 minutes. If wished, place under a preheated broiler to brown.

Spiced Pears

SPICED PEARS

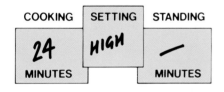

COOKING	SETTING	STANDING
24 MINUTES	HIGH	— MINUTES

2 cups hard cider or dry
   white wine
¼ cup apricot preserve,
   strained
¼ cup dark brown sugar
¼ teaspoon ground cinnamon
2 whole cloves
6 firm pears
thin strips of orange rind
juice of ½ lemon
3 tablespoons slivered almonds,
   toasted

Serves 4-6

1 Put cider, preserve, sugar and spices in a 2 quart casserole and microwave at 100% (high) for 5 minutes.
2 Peel the pears, leaving them whole and with the stems on. Cut a thin slice off the bottom of each, if necessary, so they will stand upright, and place in the casserole. Baste with the liquid.
3 Add the orange rind and lemon juice and cover with pierced plastic wrap. Microwave at 100% (high) for 9-11 minutes, or until the pears are just tender but not too soft. Give the casserole a half turn after 5 minutes. The exact cooking time will vary depending on the ripeness of the fruit.
4 Stand the pears in a serving dish. Microwave the liquid at 100% (high) for 10 minutes to reduce by half, then pour over the pears. Leave overnight to soak in the refrigerator or in a cool place. About 1 hour before serving, baste the pears well with the syrup.
5 Sprinkle the almonds over the pears just before serving.

GRASSHOPPER PIE

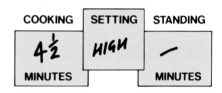

COOKING	SETTING	STANDING
4½ MINUTES	HIGH	— MINUTES

½ cup butter or margarine
2½ cups chocolate wafer
   crumbs
40 large marshmallows
⅓ cup milk
⅓ cup green Crème de Menthe
1½ cups heavy cream
few drops of green food
   coloring (optional)
angelica, to decorate

Makes a 9 inch pie

1 Place the butter in a 9 inch pie dish. Cover and microwave at until melted. Mix in the wafer crumbs and press the mixture into the pie dish.
2 Microwave at 100% (high) for 1-3 minutes, or until hot, turning once or twice. Set aside to cool.
3 In a 3 quart casserole or large bowl, combine the marshmallows and milk. Microwave at 100% (high) for 3-5 minutes, or until the marshmallows are melted, stirring frequently. Mix in the Crème de Menthe. Chill for 1-2 hours; stir occasionally.
4 Beat 1 cup of the cream and fold it into the marshmallow mixture. Add a little of the food coloring if liked. Pour into the crumb crust and return the pie to the refrigerator to chill for at least 3 hours. Just before serving, whip the remaining cream and spoon it into a pastry bag with a shell tip. Pipe a design around the top edge of the pie and decorate it with angelica leaves.

Grasshopper Pie

KIWI & GRAPE CHEESE PIE

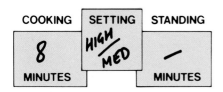

COOKING	SETTING	STANDING
8 MINUTES	HIGH / MED	— MINUTES

2 cups all-purpose flour
pinch of salt
½ cup butter or margarine, diced
3-4 tablespoons milk
For the filling:
¾ cup small curd cottage cheese
⅓ cup superfine sugar
2 teaspoons cornstarch
3 eggs

few drops vanilla
1¼ cups heavy cream
To decorate:
3 kiwi fruit, pared and sliced
purple grapes, halved and seeded

Serves 6

1 Sift the flour and salt into a bowl, then cut in the fat. Sprinkle over the milk and mix to a dough.
2 Roll out the dough on a lightly floured surface and use to line a 9 inch pie plate. Trim dough edge ¼ inch above the top of the dish to allow for shrinkage. Crimp the pastry rim.
3 Prick the side and base of the dough well with a fork. Line the base with a double sheet of

paper towels, and microwave at 100% (high) for 3 minutes, giving a quarter turn every minute. Remove paper and microwave at 100% (high) for 1-2 minutes, until cooked.
4 Beat the cheese, sugar and cornstarch together. Mix in the eggs, vanilla and cream. Microwave at 100% (high) for 4-5 minutes, or until thick, beating with a wire whip every minute. Do not overcook or the mixture will separate. If necessary, reduce power to 50% (medium) after 3 minutes, for greater control.
5 Pour the cheese filling into the pie crust. Draw a spatula back and forth over the surface. Chill for at least 2 hours. Decorate with kiwi fruit and grapes.

DATE & PECAN BAKED APPLES

COOKING	SETTING	STANDING
8 MINUTES	*HIGH*	**2** MINUTES

4 large cooking apples (about 7 oz each)
2 tablespoons butter
⅓ cup natural unsweetened apple juice
whipped cream, to serve
For the filling:
⅓ cup roughly chopped pitted dates
2 tablespoons chopped pecans
1½ tablespoons light brown sugar
½ teaspoon ground cinnamon

Serves 4

1 Using an apple corer or a small sharp knife, remove the core from each apple. Score the skin around the middle of each apple with a sharp knife.
2 To make the filling, mix the dates, pecans, sugar and cinnamon in a bowl. Use to fill the apple centers, pressing down firmly with the back of a teaspoon. Dot with butter.
3 Place the apples in a shallow casserole dish, then pour the apple juice around them. Microwave at 100% (high) for 8-9 minutes, or until apples are soft when pierced through the center with a knife. Let stand 2 minutes.
4 Serve at once with whipped cream.

TROPICAL CRUMBLE

COOKING	SETTING	STANDING
11 MINUTES	*HIGH*	**—** MINUTES

4 oranges, peeled and chopped
4 fresh apricots, pitted and chopped
2 large bananas, peeled and sliced
1 cup chopped fresh pineapple, or drained canned pineapple chunks
light cream or ice cream to serve
For the topping:
½ cup all-purpose flour
½ teaspoon ground ginger
⅓ cup quick-cooking oats
⅓ cup shredded coconut
¾ cup dark brown sugar
5 tablespoons butter

Serves 4-6

1 First make the topping. Sift the flour and ginger into a mixing bowl. Add the oats, coconut and sugar and mix together. Cut the butter in pieces, place in a small bowl and microwave at 100% (high) for 50-60 seconds to melt. Stir into the topping mix and turn so that all the dry ingredients are coated with the butter.
2 Put all the fruit into a deep microproof glass dish, turning the bananas in the juice from the oranges to prevent them discoloring.
3 Sprinkle the topping evenly over the fruit and press down gently to level the surface. Microwave at 100% (high) for 10-12 minutes, giving the dish a quarter turn every 3 minutes.
4 Serve hot with cream or ice cream.

Tropical Crumble

APRICOT & NUT SPONGE PUDDING

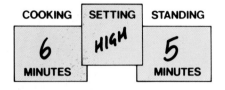

COOKING	SETTING	STANDING
6 MINUTES	**HIGH**	**5** MINUTES

⅔ cup dried apricots
½ cup margarine or butter
½ cup superfine sugar
2 eggs, lightly beaten
few drops of almond extract
1½ cups self-rising flour
pinch of salt
½ cup coarsely chopped walnuts

3 tablespoons milk
For the sauce:
4-5 tablespoons apricot preserve
1 teaspoon lemon juice

Serves 4-6

1 Grease a 4 cup pudding mold or line with plastic wrap. Wash the apricots and cut them in small even-sized pieces with kitchen shears. Set aside.

2 Beat the margarine with the sugar until light and fluffy. Add the beaten eggs, a little at a time, beating after each addition. Thoroughly stir in a few drops of almond extract.

3 Sift the flour and salt together, then using a metal spoon, lightly fold into the creamed mixture alternately with the apricots and walnuts. Stir in the milk.

4 Spoon the batter into the prepared pudding mold and smooth the top. Cover the pudding mold with pierced plastic wrap and then microwave the pudding at 100% (high) for 5-6 minutes, giving the mold a half turn after 3 minutes.

5 Let stand for 5-10 minutes, before serving. Meanwhile place preserve in a small bowl with lemon juice. Stir and microwave at 100% (high) for 45-60 seconds to heat.

6 Invert the pudding on a warmed serving platter. Pour the sauce over pudding and serve piping hot.

Apricot & Nut Sponge Pudding

SURPRISE MERINGUE PIE

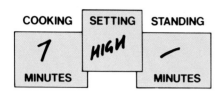

COOKING	SETTING	STANDING
1	HIGH	—
MINUTES		MINUTES

pastry for 1 (9 inch)
  pie shell
For the filling:
½ cup butter
⅓ cup light brown sugar
¼ cup superfine sugar
1 small can (5 oz) sweetened
  condensed milk
2 extra-large egg yolks
For the meringue:
2 extra-large egg whites ·
½ cup superfine sugar

Serves 4-6

1 Roll out the dough and use to line a 9 inch round pie dish. Take the edge ¼ inch above the rim, to allow for shrinkage, and crimp. Prick side and base. Line base with a double sheet of paper towels. Microwave at 100% (high) for 1-2 minutes, turning several times.
2 To make the filling, put the butter, sugar and milk in a 1½ quart bowl and microwave at 100% (high) for 4 minutes, stirring every 2 minutes. Beat in yolks and pour into the pie crust.
3 Beat the egg whites until stiff, beat in half the sugar and fold in the rest. Swirl meringue over the filling to cover. Microwave at 100% (high) for 2 minutes. Brown under a preheated broiler.

PEACH & RICE CONDE

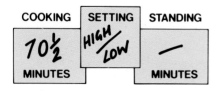

COOKING	SETTING	STANDING
70½	HIGH/LOW	—
MINUTES		MINUTES

Surprise Meringue Pie

½ cup short-grain rice, rinsed
  and well drained
3 tablespoons sugar
4 cups milk
1¼ cups heavy cream
½ teaspoon vanilla
4 tablespoons raspberry preserve
1 can (16 oz) peach halves, well
  drained

Serves 4-6

1 Put the rice, sugar and milk in a large bowl and microwave at 100% (high) for 10 minutes, or until almost boiling, stirring occasionally.
2 Reduce power to 30% (low) and microwave for 60-70 minutes, or until almost all of the milk is absorbed, stirring every 15 minutes. Cover closely with plastic wrap to prevent a skin from forming and let cool completely.
3 Whip the cream to soft peaks.

Fold half into the cold rice with the vanilla. Spoon the rice and cream mixture into a serving dish and level the surface.
4 Strain raspberry preserve into a small bowl and microwave at 100% (high) for 30-40 seconds, or until melted.
5 Arrange the peach halves, cut side down, in a circle on top of the rice, leaving a border around the edge. Brush the peaches with warmed preserve. Pipe the remaining cream around the edge of the rice and in the center. Serve cold.

ICE CREAM VARIETY

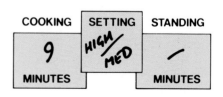

COOKING	SETTING	STANDING
9	HIGH/MED	—
MINUTES		MINUTES

1 egg
2 egg yolks
6 tablespoons superfine sugar
1¼ cups milk
½ teaspoon vanilla
1¼ cups heavy cream
vanilla wafers (optional)

Serves 6

1 Place the egg and egg yolks in a 2 quart bowl with the sugar and beat until pale and creamy.
2 In a 4 cup liquid measure, microwave the milk at 100% (high) for 1-2 minutes. Beat into the egg mixture.
3 Microwave at 50% (medium) for 8 minutes, until the custard is lightly thickened. Stir every 2 minutes and then 3-4 times in the last minute. Stir in the vanilla, cover with plastic wrap and let cool completely.
4 Whip the cream until just thick enough to hold its shape. Fold into the custard. Pour into a freezerproof container. Cover and freeze for 1 hour, or until frozen about ½ inch around the sides.
5 Turn the mixture into a bowl and beat thoroughly to break up the ice crystals. Return to container, cover and freeze for 1-2 hours more until firm. Soften at room temperature for 10 minutes before serving. Scoop into stemware and serve with vanilla wafers if liked.

To flavor, fold one of the following into custard before freezing.

Hazelnut: Add 1 cup chopped toasted hazelnuts.

Chocolate: Mix 2 tablespoons unsweetened cocoa with 1 tablespoon boiling water and add.

Ripple: Swirl 2 tablespoons strained raspberries through the mixture after breaking up the ice crystals. Do not overmix.

Berry: Add 1½ cups crushed berries, sweetened to taste.

Peach & Rice Condé

Raspberry Mold

4 Meanwhile dissolve the other package of gelatin in a 4 cup measure with ⅔ cup hot water at 100% (high) for 30 seconds. Stir and add ⅔ cup cold water and mix. Whip the cream into the cool but still liquid gelatin and pour over the banana gelatin. Refrigerate until set.

5 Dip the mold in a bowl of hot water for 1-2 seconds, then invert on a dampened plate. Serve.

BROWN BREAD ICE CREAM

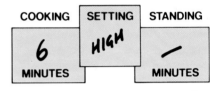

COOKING	SETTING	STANDING
6 MINUTES	HIGH	— MINUTES

*2 eggs plus 2 egg
   whites
2 cups milk
¾ cup sugar
1 tablespoon dark rum
1¼ cups heavy cream
2 cups brown bread crumbs,
   toasted
a selection of crisp
   cookies*

Serves 4-6

1 Place the whole eggs, milk and sugar in a bowl and mix well. Microwave at 100% (high) for 6 minutes, stirring every 3 minutes, until the custard mixture is smooth and slightly thickened. Set aside to cool.

2 Mix in the rum and cream. Pour into a large freezer container and freeze until almost firm (about 1½ hours).

3 Remove the half-frozen ice cream from the freezer and spoon into a bowl. Beat until the ice-cream mixture is completely smooth and free from any large ice crystals.

4 In a spotlessly clean and dry bowl, using clean beaters, beat the egg whites to stiff peaks. Fold

RASPBERRY MOLD

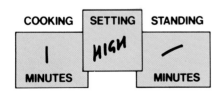

COOKING	SETTING	STANDING
1 MINUTES	HIGH	— MINUTES

*2 packages (3 oz) raspberry-
   flavoured gelatin
3 small bananas
1-2 tablespoons lemon juice
1¼ cups heavy cream*

Serves 6

1 Rinse out a 5 cup metal gelatin mold with cold water, shake off the excess moisture and place it in the refrigerator to chill.

2 Place ⅔ cup hot water in a 4 cup measure and stir in 1 package gelatin. Microwave at 100% (high) for 30 seconds to dissolve. Stir, then make up to 2½ cups with cold water. Refrigerate until thick but not set.

3 Peel and slice the bananas, toss in lemon juice, then fold into the thick gelatin. Spoon into the chilled mold, and refrigerate until firm but slightly sticky to the touch.

into the ice cream with the bread crumbs, using a large spoon. Return to the container and freeze for 3-4 hours until firm. Serve the ice cream in chilled sundae dishes with crisp cookies.

CHOCOLATE BANANA POPS

COOKING	SETTING	STANDING
2 MINUTES	HIGH	— MINUTES

2 bananas
1 bar (4 oz) sweet German chocolate, broken in squares
1 tablespoon margarine or butter
1 cup chopped walnuts (optional)

Serves 8

1 Cut the bananas across in 4 equal pieces, then push a wooden cocktail pick into the side of each piece. Wrap in foil and freeze for about 6 hours or until firm.
2 Put the chocolate and mar- garine into a bowl and micro- wave at 100% (high) for 2-3 minutes, or until melted, stirring midway through this time.
3 Remove the bananas from the freezer. Holding each piece by a pick, dip into the chocolate mix- ture, and turn it quickly to coat on all sides. If necessary, use a spoon to complete this covering, and to scrape off any excess.
4 Quickly roll each pop in chop- ped nuts, if using, then insert the cocktail pick in a grapefruit or melon. Leave for a few minutes until set, then serve.

Chocolate Banana Pops

91

C·A·K·E·S

Chocolate Nut Triangles

CHOCOLATE NUT TRIANGLES

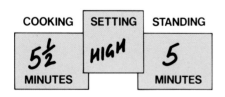

COOKING	SETTING	STANDING
5½ MINUTES	HIGH	5 MINUTES

¾ cup all-purpose flour
¼ cup unsweetened cocoa
½ teaspoon baking powder
pinch of salt
6 tablespoons margarine

½ cup light brown sugar
¼ cup light corn syrup
¼ teaspoon vanilla
2 eggs, lightly beaten
2 tablespoons milk
3 tablespoons canned
  chocolate frosting
chopped toasted hazelnuts

Makes 8

1 Grease an 8 inch square cake dish and line the base with greased waxed paper.
2 Sift the flour, cocoa, baking powder and salt together into a large bowl.
3 Beat the margarine, sugar and syrup together until pale and creamy, then beat in the vanilla. Beat in the eggs, stir in the flour mixture and milk and beat briefly until smooth and evenly blended.
4 Pour the batter into the prepared dish and level the surface. Cover the corners of the dish with small smooth triangles of foil. (Check your oven handbook to ensure that small pieces of foil may be used for protection.)

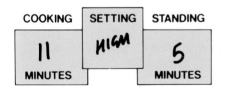

M·I·C·R·O·T·I·P

Toasted almonds make an attractive decoration or topping for desserts. Spread slivered or split almonds on a flat plate and microwave at 100% (high) for 5-7 minutes, stirring or shaking several times, until browned. Brown at least ¾ cup at a time. Toast hazelnuts in the same way.

5 Microwave at 100% (high) for 5½-6½ minutes, giving a quarter turn every 2 minutes. Let stand 5 minutes, then run a slim spatula around the side, invert on a wire rack and peel off the lining paper. Turn the right way up and let cool completely.

6 To finish, trim off any rough edges, cover the top of the cake with the frosting and cut the cake in 4 squares. Cut each square into 2 triangles.

7 Decorate the tops with chopped hazelnuts.

MOCHA GATEAU

COOKING	SETTING	STANDING
11 MINUTES	HIGH	5 MINUTES

6 tablespoons butter
½ cup superfine sugar
4 large eggs, separated
1 tablespoon milk
5 squares (5 oz) semisweet chocolate, roughly grated
¾ cup plus 2 tablespoons presifted all-purpose flour

For the icing and decoration:
¼ cup cornstarch
¾ cup light brown sugar
1¼ cups milk
1½ tablespoons instant coffee granules
1 cup butter

Mocha Gateau

¼ cup chopped nutmeats
4 squares (4 oz) semisweet chocolate
confectioner's sugar
6-8 coffee beans

Serves 6-8

1 Beat the butter with half the superfine sugar until light and fluffy. Beat in the yolks one by one, and add the milk. Place the chocolate in a small bowl and microwave at 100% (high) for 1-1½ minutes, stirring after 1 minute, to melt. Stir into batter.

2 Beat the egg whites until stiff, then beat in the remaining sugar. Fold into the chocolate-flavored batter, then fold in the flour. Pour into a greased 8 inch cake dish or soufflé mold lined with greased waxed paper.

3 Place in the oven on top of an upturned plate and microwave at 100% (high) for 7-8 minutes, turning every 1½-2 minutes. Let stand for 5 minutes before inverting on a wire rack. Peel off the paper and let cool.

4 To make the coffee icing, mix cornstarch and sugar to a paste with ¼ cup milk. Place the remaining milk in a liquid measure with the coffee and microwave at 100% (high) for 2-3 minutes, or until boiling. Add to the cornstarch mixture, stir and microwave at 100% (high) for 1 minute or until thick. Cover with wet waxed paper and leave until cold.

5 Beat the butter until creamy. Beat in the coffee mixture. Reserve 8 tablespoons in a pastry bag fitted with a large star tip.

6 Split the cake in three layers. Use the remaining icing to sandwich the layers together and to coat the top side. Press nuts around the side.

7 Using a vegetable parer, shave curls from the back of the chocolate squares and arrange on top of the cake. Lay strips of waxed paper across the curls. Sift confectioner's sugar on top, then remove paper. Pipe a border of cream around the top and bottom edges. Decorate with coffee beans.

Frosted Walnut Cake

FROSTED WALNUT CAKE

COOKING	SETTING	STANDING
6 MINUTES	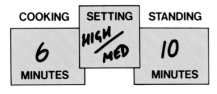 HIGH/MED	**10** MINUTES

¾ cup margarine or butter
1½ cups self-rising flour
¾ cup superfine sugar
3 eggs, beaten
¼-⅓ cup milk
¼ teaspoon imitation black
  walnut extract
¾ cup chopped walnuts
8 walnut halves, to decorate
For the frosting:
2 tablespoons butter
2 tablespoons light cream or milk
pinch of salt
2⅔ cups confectioner's sugar
a few drops of vanilla

Serves 8

1 Beat together the margarine, flour, superfine sugar, eggs and sufficient milk to give a soft dropping consistency. Fold in the walnut extract and chopped walnuts.
2 Grease an 8 inch cake dish and line the base with greased waxed paper. Spoon the cake batter into the dish.
3 Microwave at 100% (high) for 5½-6½ minutes, or until a skewer inserted in the center comes out clean. Give the dish a half turn every 2 minutes.
4 Let stand for 10 minutes, then invert out on a wire rack, remove the lining paper and let cool. Cut in 2 layers.
5 To make the frosting, combine the butter and 1½ tablespoons of the cream or milk with the salt in a mixing bowl. Microwave at 50% (medium) for 30-40 seconds, or until bubbling. Add the confectioner's sugar and beat until the frosting is smooth. Add the vanilla and a little more cream or milk if necessary to make a spreading consistency.
6 Place one cake half on a serving platter and spread with a little frosting. Put the remaining layer on top. Pile the frosting on top and quickly spread it over the top and side with a slim spatula. Mark into decorative swirls.
7 Gently press walnut halves around the cake top before the frosting sets. Leave to set before serving.

PARTY FANCIES & CUPCAKE CATS

COOKING	SETTING	STANDING
3 MINUTES	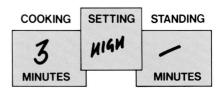 HIGH	**—** MINUTES

¼ cup margarine or butter
⅓ cup light brown sugar
1 egg, lightly beaten
grated rind of 1 orange
½ cup self-rising flour
¼ teaspoon baking powder
1 tablespoon milk
2 teaspoons lemon juice
To decorate the fancies:
¼ cup confectioner's sugar
a few drops of lemon juice
1-2 drops yellow food coloring
12-14 candied fruit slices
To decorate the cats:
¼ cup confectioner's sugar
a few drops of orange juice
1-2 drops orange food coloring
12-14 cinnamon nonpareils
  for eyes
6-7 small candied orange or
  lemon slices, halved, for ears
6-7 jelly beans for noses
1 square (1 oz) semisweet
  chocolate, melted

Makes 12-14

1 Beat the margarine and sugar together until pale and fluffy. Beat in the egg and orange rind.

2 Sift the flour and baking powder together, and fold in with the milk and lemon juice.

3 Place 6-7 double thickness cupcake papers in a ring around the edge of a plate and half fill each case with the cake batter, spreading it as evenly as possible.

4 Microwave at 100% (high) for 1½-2 minutes, giving the plate a half turn after 1 minute. Place on a wire rack to cool. Repeat with the remaining batter.

5 To decorate the party fancies, blend the confectioner's sugar with the lemon juice and yellow coloring to make lemon icing. Top 6-7 cakes and decorate with orange and lemon slices.

6 For the cupcake cats, mix the confectioner's sugar with a few drops of orange juice and orange coloring to make icing. Use to coat the remaining cakes. While soft, position eyes, ears and noses.

7 Place the chocolate in a small pastry bag fitted with a writing tip and pipe whiskers and mouths.

LEMON GATEAU

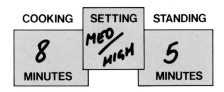

COOKING	SETTING	STANDING
8 MINUTES	MED/HIGH	*5* MINUTES

½ cup butter
½ cup superfine sugar
2 eggs
1 cup self-rising flour
1 teaspoon baking powder
1½ tablespoons lemon juice
1 tablespoon milk
For the filling:
2 tablespoons butter
1 tablespoon lemon juice
2-3 teaspoons milk
1 teaspoon grated lemon rind
1⅔ cup confectioner's sugar
2-3 drops yellow food
 coloring
For the topping:
1 cup heavy cream, lightly
 whipped
candied lemon slices

Serves 6

1 Line the base of a 9 x 5 inch loaf dish and lightly grease.

2 Beat the butter and sugar together until light and creamy. Gradually beat in the eggs.

3 Sift the flour and baking powder together and add to the mixture with the lemon juice and milk. Combine with a metal spoon. Spoon into the prepared dish and level the surface with a spoon.

4 Microwave at 50% (medium) for 7-8 minutes, giving a quarter turn every 2 minutes. Microwave for 1 minute at 100% (high) to finish cooking, if necessary. The cake is cooked when a skewer inserted in the center comes out clean.

5 Let stand for 5 minutes, then invert on a wire rack, remove the lining paper and leave the cake to cool completely.

6 To make the filling, combine the butter, lemon juice, milk and grated lemon rind in a bowl. Microwave at 50% (medium) for 1-2 minutes, or until bubbling. Add the confectioner's sugar and coloring and beat until smooth and of spreading consistency. Add more milk if the mixture is too thick.

7 Cut the cake horizontally in 4 layers and sandwich together with the filling.

8 Place the cake on a serving platter and coat the top and side with whipped cream, using a slim spatula to give a swirled effect. Decorate with lemon slices. Chill in the refrigerator until ready to serve.

Lemon Gateau

M·I·C·R·O·T·I·P

When baking cakes in a microwave oven, more even cooking can be achieved by standing the dish on an inverted plate in the oven. This allows the microwaves to penetrate from below.

ORANGE RING CAKE

COOKING	SETTING	STANDING
6½ MINUTES	*HIGH*	**5** MINUTES

1½ cups all-purpose flour
2½ teaspoons baking powder
¾ cup margarine, softened
1 cup packed light brown sugar
3 eggs, lightly beaten
grated rind and juice of 1 orange
3-4 tablespoons milk
For the icing and decoration:
2¼ cups confectioner's sugar
grated rind of 1 orange
3 tablespoons orange juice
1 square (1 oz) semisweet
   chocolate, broken into pieces
thin slices of orange

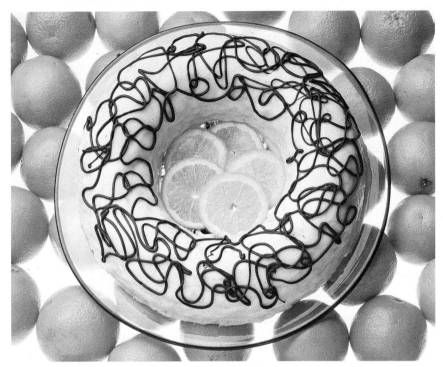

Orange Ring Cake

Serves 10-12

1 Lightly grease a 9 inch glass cake ring mold.
2 Sift the flour and baking powder together into a large bowl. Add the margarine, sugar, eggs and orange rind and juice and beat for 2-3 minutes until blended. Add enough milk to form a soft dropping consistency.
3 Spoon the batter into the prepared ring and level the surface. Microwave at 100% (high) for 5½-6 minutes, or until a skewer inserted in the center comes out clean. Give the dish a quarter turn every 2 minutes.
4 Let stand for 5 minutes, then invert on a wire rack.
5 To make the icing, sift the confectioner's sugar into a bowl. Blend in the orange rind and juice.
6 Place a large plate underneath the wire rack. Pour the icing over the top of the cake and quickly spread it over the side with a spatula. Leave to set.
7 Put the chocolate into a 2 cup bowl and microwave at 100%

(high) for 45-60 seconds to melt, stirring twice.
8 Put the melted chocolate into a waxed paper pastry bag, snip off the tip and pipe squiggly lines over the iced cake. Place on a plate and arrange orange slices in the center.

CHOCOLATE CRUNCH

COOKING	SETTING	STANDING
1 MINUTES	*HIGH/MED*	**10** MINUTES

⅔ cup butter or margarine
½ cup light brown sugar
¼ cup light corn syrup
2 cups crispy rice cereal
1 cup quick-cooking oats
¼ cup chopped mixed
   nuts
6 squares (6 oz) semisweet
   chocolate, broken in
   pieces

Makes 16 squares

1 Grease a shallow 8 inch square dish and line the base with rice paper.
2 Put the butter, sugar and syrup in a 2 quart bowl and microwave at 100% (high) for 2-3 minutes, stirring once or twice, until melted. Watch to make certain the contents do not boil over.
3 Stir the crispy rice cereal, oats and mixed nuts into the bowl. Spread mixture in the greased dish and level with a dampened large metal spoon.
4 Microwave at 100% (high) for 3-3½ minutes, giving the dish a quarter turn every minute. Cool for 10 minutes.
5 Put the chocolate in a 2 cup measure with 2 tablespoons cold water. Microwave at 50% (medium) for 2-3 minutes or until melted, stirring 2-3 times.
6 Using a spatula, spread the melted chocolate over the crunch. Leave for 5 minutes, then make a wavy pattern on the top with a fork. Mark into squares. Let stand in refrigerator until firm, then cut into 16 squares and serve.

BLACK FOREST GATEAU

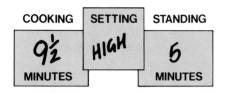

COOKING	SETTING	STANDING
9½ MINUTES	HIGH	5 MINUTES

6 tablespoons butter
½ cup superfine sugar
4 large eggs, separated
1 tablespoon milk
5 squares (5 oz) semisweet
    chocolate, grated
¾ cup plus 2 tablespoons
    all-purpose flour, sifted

For the filling and decoration:
1 can (16 oz) pitted Bing
    cherries, drained with
    ⅓ cup syrup reserved
1 teaspoon cornstarch
½ cup Kirsch
2 cups heavy cream
3 tablespoons superfine sugar
1 square (1 oz) semisweet
    chocolate, roughly grated

Serves 8

1 Lightly grease an 8 inch round cake dish and line the base with greased waxed paper.
2 Beat the butter with half the sugar until light and fluffy. Add the egg yolks, one by one, and mix thoroughly. Add the milk and stir so that all the ingredients are well blended.
3 Place the chocolate in a small bowl and microwave at 100% (high) for 1½ minutes to melt, stirring after 1 minute. Stir into the creamed mixture.
4 Beat the egg whites until stiff, then beat in the remaining sugar. Fold into the chocolate mixture, then fold in the flour.
5 Put the mixture into the prepared dish and place in the oven on top of an inverted plate. Microwave at 100% (high) for 7-8 minutes, turning every 1½-2 minutes.
6 Let stand 5 minutes, then invert on a wire rack, remove paper.
7 Pat the cherries dry with paper towels and reserve 8 for the decoration. Mix the cornstarch with the reserved cherry juice. Microwave at 100% (high) for 1-1½ minutes or until thick, stirring 2-3 times. Add ¼ cup of the Kirsch and mix.
8 Whip the heavy cream into soft peaks and beat in the superfine sugar. Fold in the remaining Kirsch. Set aside 3-4 tablespoons whipped cream for decoration.
9 To assemble the cake, split the sponge horizontally in 4 layers. Sprinkle one third of the syrup over the bottom layer, cover with about a fourth of the cream, and press half the fruit into the cream. Cover with a second layer, sprinkle with more syrup, a layer of cream, and the rest of the cherries. Lay the third cake layer on top, sprinkle with the remaining syrup and cover with more whipped cream. Top with the last cake layer and spread the remaining cream over the top and side.
10 Scatter grated chocolate over the top and pipe rosettes of cream around the edge. Top every other rosette with a cherry. Chill for 1 hour before serving.

Black Forest Gateau

CHOCOLATE CARAMEL BARS

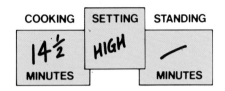

COOKING	SETTING	STANDING
14½ MINUTES	HIGH	╱ MINUTES

1½ cups all-purpose flour
pinch of salt
⅓ cup rice flour
⅔ cup margarine or butter
¼ cup superfine sugar
For the filling:
½ cup margarine
⅓ cup superfine sugar
1 tablespoon light corn syrup
1 can (14 oz) sweetened
    condensed milk
For the topping:
6 squares (6 oz) semisweet or
    German sweet chocolate

Makes 12

1 Line an 11 x 7 inch microproof dish with plastic wrap. Sift the flour into a bowl and add the salt and rice flour. Cut in the fat until it resembles fine bread crumbs. Stir in the sugar, and knead to form a dough. Press into the prepared dish, and smooth the top with back of a metal spoon. Prick well.
2 Microwave at 100% (high) for 3-4 minutes, giving the dish a quarter turn every minute. Remove from oven and let cool.
3 To make the filling, place all the ingredients in a very large bowl, to allow room for boiling. Microwave at 100% (high) for 4 minutes, stirring 2-3 times to dissolve the sugar.
4 Microwave at 100% (high) for a further 5 minutes, or until light golden brown. Stir 2-3 times. Watch to make sure it does not boil over.
5 Pour over pie crust and let cool.

6 Break the chocolate in pieces and place in a bowl. Microwave at 100% (high) for 2½-3½ minutes, or until melted, stirring 2-3 times. Spread over the caramel. Mark in bars and leave to set for a few minutes before removing the bars from the dish.

HONEY TEACAKE

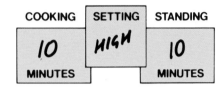

COOKING	SETTING	STANDING
10 MINUTES	HIGH	10 MINUTES

1 cup self-rising flour
1 teaspoon ground cinnamon
1 teaspoon apple pie spice
1 teaspoon baking soda
1 cup Graham flour
⅔ cup honey
grated rind and juice of
    1 orange
½ cup oil

Chocolate Caramel Bars

½ cup dark brown sugar
2 eggs, well beaten
¼ cup slivered almonds

Makes 16 slices

1 Lightly grease an 8 x 12 inch rectangular glass baking dish and line the base with waxed paper. Grease the paper.
2 Sift the self-rising flour with the ground spices and soda into a large bowl. Stir in the Graham flour.
3 Pour the honey into a bowl. Measure the orange juice and make up to ⅔ cup with boiling water, then stir into the honey. Stir in the orange rind, oil, sugar and eggs.
4 Pour the honey mixture onto the flour mixture and mix thoroughly to make a smooth batter. Pour into the prepared dish.
5 Sprinkle the surface of the mixture with almonds and microwave at 100% (high) for 10-11 minutes, giving the dish a quarter turn every 2 minutes. Stand in the dish for 10 minutes, then invert on a wire rack. Peel off the lining paper, turn the right way up and let cool.

LEMON TOP CUPCAKES

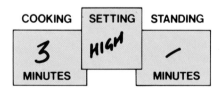

COOKING	SETTING	STANDING
3 MINUTES	HIGH	**1** MINUTES

¼ cup soft butter or margarine
⅓ cup light brown sugar
1 egg, lightly beaten
finely grated rind of 1 lemon
½ cup self-rising flour
¼ teaspoon baking powder
1 tablespoon milk
For the icing and decoration:
1-2 tablespoons lemon curd
1-2 tablespoons black currant or grape preserve

Lemon Top Cupcakes

3 tablespoons soft butter
⅔ cup sifted confectioner's sugar
1 teaspoon milk
6-7 small candied lemon slices

Makes 12-14

1 Beat the fat and sugar together until pale and fluffy. Add the eggs a little at a time, beating thoroughly after each addition. Beat in the lemon rind.
2 Sift the flour and baking powder together, and fold into the batter with the milk.
3 Place 6-7 double thickness cupcake papers in a ring around the edge of a plate. Half-fill each cupcake paper with cake batter, spreading it as evenly as possible.

4 Microwave at 100% (high) for 1½-2 minutes, giving the plate a quarter turn after 1 minute. Place cakes on a wire rack to cool. Repeat with remaining batter.
5 Spread the top of half the cakes with lemon curd and the other half with black currant or grape preserve, taking the curd and preserve almost to the edge of each cake.
6 To mix the buttercream, beat the butter until very soft, then beat in the confectioner's sugar and milk. Place in a pastry bag fitted with a star tip and pipe a border of stars around the top edge of each cake.
7 Decorate each lemon cake with a candied lemon slice. Serve the cakes as soon as possible.

MICROWAVE LAYER CAKE

COOKING	SETTING	STANDING
5½ MINUTES	HIGH	10 MINUTES

1½ cups self-rising flour
pinch of salt
¾ cup soft butter
¾ cup superfine sugar
3 large eggs, lightly beaten
2-3 tablespoons milk
vegetable oil for greasing
For the filling:
3-4 tablespoons red preserve
⅔ cup heavy cream, optional
superfine or confectioner's
   sugar, to decorate

Serves 8

1 Line the base of a 8 inch cake dish or soufflé mold with waxed paper, then lightly grease the paper.

2 Sift the flour and salt together and set aside. Beat the butter and sugar together until light and creamy. Add the eggs a little at a time, beating thoroughly after each addition. Fold in the sifted flour, about one third at a time, using a metal spoon. Fold in the milk.

3 Place in prepared dish and microwave at 100% (high) for 5½-6½ minutes, until a skewer inserted in the center comes out clean. Give the dish a quarter turn every 2 minutes, for even cooking.

4 Let stand for 10 minutes, then invert on a wire rack, remove lining paper, turn the right way up and let cool completely.

5 Split the cake in half. Spread 1 half with preserve. Whip cream until thick, if using, and spread over the cut side of the other half. Sandwich together and sift superfine or confectioner's sugar over the top.

Microwave Layer Cake

6 Place on a serving platter, and serve within 2 hours.

Orange Layer: Sandwich layers together with marmalade and cream. Top with whipped cream and decorate with mandarin orange sections.

Coconut Layer: Sandwich layers together with cherry preserve. Mix 1 cup confectioner's sugar with 1 tablespoon warm water and use to ice the top of the cake. While still soft, scatter the top thickly with shredded coconut; arrange sliced candied cherries around the top edge.

Chocolate Layer: Replace ¼ cup of the flour with unsweetened cocoa. Sandwich cake together with whipped cream. Sift confectioner's sugar over the top, then pipe a lattice of melted chocolate cake covering.

CHOCOLATE CAKE

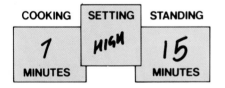

COOKING	SETTING	STANDING
1 MINUTES	HIGH	*15* MINUTES

½ cup margarine
1¾ cups self-rising flour
2 tablespoons unsweetened cocoa
pinch of salt
1 cup superfine sugar
2 large eggs
⅓ cup evaporated milk
⅓ cup water
1 teaspoon vanilla
For the filling and topping:
1¾ cups confectioner's sugar
⅓ cup sweetened cocoa
5 tablespoons margarine
3 tablespoons milk
1 teaspoon vanilla
2 individual bags M & M candies

Makes 8-10 slices

Chocolate Cake

1 Lightly grease an 8 inch soufflé mold or cake dish and line the base with waxed paper, then grease the paper.

2 Place the margarine, cut into pieces, in a small bowl and microwave at 100% (high) for 1-1½ minutes to melt.

3 Sift the flour, cocoa and salt into a large bowl. Stir in the sugar, then make a well in the center. Beat the eggs with the milk, water and vanilla, then add to the dry ingredients together with the margarine and beat until blended.

4 Spoon the batter into the prepared mold, then microwave at 100% (high) for 5-7 minutes or until the skewer inserted in the center comes out clean, giving a quarter turn every 2 minutes.

5 Cool the cake for a few minutes, then invert on a wire rack, and peel off the lining paper. Turn the cake the right way up and leave to cool.

6 To make the filling and topping, sift the confectioner's sugar and sweetened cocoa into a bowl. Place the margarine, milk and vanilla in a small bowl and microwave at 100% (high) for 45-60 seconds to melt. Beat into sugar mixture. Let stand for 15-30 minutes to thicken.

7 Split the cake in half and spread one half with the chocolate mixture. Place the other layer on top and spread with remaining mixture. Decorate the top with M & M candies. Leave the cake for 30 minutes, to firm, before cutting.

CHAPTER NINE

E·A·S·Y E·N·T·E·R·T·A·I·N·I·N·G
C·A·N·D·L·E·L·I·T D·I·N·N·E·R

Celery Hearts Vinaigrette ● Salmon Steaks & Watercress Sauce
Zucchini au Gratin ● Passionfruit Creams – Serves 2

COUNTDOWN

In the morning:
1 Prepare the Passionfruit Creams but do not decorate.
2 Make the Celery Hearts Vinaigrette but do not garnish.
40 minutes before serving:
1 Decorate the Passionfruit Creams.

2 Garnish the celery hearts.
3 Cook the zucchini but do not top with cream, etc.
4 Cook the salmon steaks.
5 Make the watercress sauce.
6 Serve the Celery Hearts Vinaigrette.
7 Between courses, reheat the zucchini at 100% (high) for 1 minute. Top with cream, seasonings and cheese and place under a preheated broiler.
8 Meanwhile, reheat the salmon at 100% (high) for 30 seconds, then garnish.
9 Reheat the watercress sauce at 100% (high) for 30-60 seconds. Serve with the salmon and Zucchini au Gratin.

CELERY HEARTS VINAIGRETTE

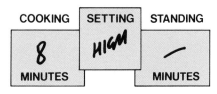

COOKING	SETTING	STANDING
8 MINUTES	HIGH	— MINUTES

2 celery hearts, washed
1¼ cups hot vegetable stock
For the vinaigrette:
¼-⅓ cup oil
2 tablespoons wine vinegar
1 tablespoon chopped fresh parsley
1 tablespoon chopped celery leaves
½ teaspoon dried mixed herbs
1 clove garlic, crushed
1 teaspoon Dijon mustard
salt and pepper
For the garnish:
1 hard-cooked egg
canned pimiento
chopped fresh parsley

1 Trim the celery hearts to about 6 inches long.
2 Place the hearts side-by-side in a shallow dish and pour over the boiling stock. Cover with pierced plastic wrap and microwave at 100% (high) for 8-10 minutes, turning the celery once.

3 Meanwhile, to make the vinaigrette, beat together all the ingredients.
4 Drain the stock from the celery and reserve for making the watercress sauce to serve with the salmon.
5 Spoon the vinaigrette dressing over the celery hearts, then chill in the refrigerator for 3-4 hours.
6 To garnish, cut the egg in half. Scoop out and strain the yolk and slice the white in two.
7 Use a small heart-shaped cutter, about ½ inch in diameter, to cut a few hearts from the egg white and pimiento.
8 To serve, place the celery on individual plates, spoon the dressing over, sprinkle with egg yolk and parsley, then top with the egg white and pimiento hearts.

SALMON STEAKS & WATERCRESS SAUCE

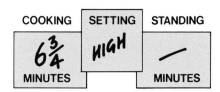

COOKING	SETTING	STANDING
6¾ MINUTES	HIGH	— MINUTES

2 salmon steaks (about ½ lb each)
lemon juice
3 tablespoons butter
salt and pepper
¾ cup pared, seeded and sliced cucumber
1 cup finely chopped watercress
1 tablespoon all-purpose flour
⅔ cup stock from Celery Hearts Vinaigrette or vegetable stock
parsley sprigs and lemon slices, for garnish

1 Lay the salmon steaks in a shallow dish, sprinkle with a little lemon juice and dot with 1 tablespoon butter.
2 Cover with pierced plastic wrap and microwave at 100%

(high) for 2½-3½ minutes, or until the fish flakes easily when tested with a fork. Season with salt and pepper to taste.

3 Place the cucumber in a small bowl, cover with pierced plastic wrap and microwave at 100% (high) for 1 minute. Drain thoroughly.

4 Place the watercress in a small bowl with 2 teaspoons water, cover with pierced plastic wrap and microwave at 100% (high) for 1 minute. Drain and let cool.

5 Beat 1 tablespoon butter until soft, then beat in the watercress.

6 Place the remaining butter in a 3 cup bowl and microwave at 100% (high) for 20-30 seconds to melt. Stir in the flour, then gradually add the stock, stirring continuously.

7 Microwave at 100% (high) for 2 minutes, or until thick, stirring 2-3 times. Add the watercress butter and stir well. Stir in the cucumber and season to taste with salt and pepper.

8 Remove and discard the skin from the salmon, place on a hot serving dish and garnish with parsley and halved lemon slices. Serve the watercress sauce separately in a warmed sauceboat, and accompany with new potatoes, if liked.

ZUCCHINI AU GRATIN

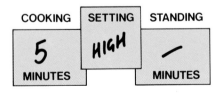

COOKING	SETTING	STANDING
5 MINUTES	HIGH	— MINUTES

3 cups sliced zucchini
salt and pepper
3 tablespoons heavy cream
pinch of grated nutmeg
2 tablespoons grated Parmesan
  cheese

1 Place the zucchini in a shallow serving dish. Add 2 tablespoons

water, cover with pierced plastic wrap and microwave at 100% (high) for 5-7 minutes. Give the dish a half turn and stir after 3 minutes.

2 Drain the zucchini and season with salt and pepper. Spoon the cream over them and season again with salt, pepper and nutmeg. Sprinkle with cheese.

3 Place under a preheated broiler to brown.

PASSIONFRUIT CREAMS

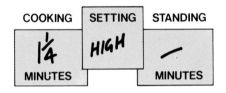

COOKING	SETTING	STANDING
1¼ MINUTES	HIGH	— MINUTES

12 passionfruit
3 tablespoons superfine sugar
1¾ teaspoons unflavored gelatin
⅔ cup heavy cream
1 small egg white
3 squares (3 oz) semisweet
  chocolate, grated

1 Cut 8 passionfruit in half, scoop out the pulp and press through a strainer to extract the juice. Discard the seeds. Make

the juice up to ⅓ cup with water.

2 Place 1 tablespoon sugar, 1 tablespoon water and 1 teaspoon gelatin in a small bowl. Leave for 5 minutes, then microwave at 100% (high) for 10-15 seconds to melt. Do not boil.

3 Stir in the fruit juice and pour into 2 glasses. Tilt on their sides in the refrigerator. Leave for 1-2 hours to set.

4 Sprinkle the remaining gelatin over 1 tablespoon water in a small bowl and let stand for 5 minutes. Meanwhile, halve the remaining passion fruit, scoop out the pulp and reserve.

5 Whip half the cream to soft peaks. Beat the egg white until stiff, beat in the remaining sugar, and continue beating until stiff.

6 Microwave the gelatin at 100% (high) for 10-15 seconds to melt. Stir in the passion fruit pulp. Add a little of this mixture to the egg whites and fold in gently. Fold in the remaining mixture until no trace of egg white remains.

7 Fold in the whipped cream, spoon into the glasses and return to the refrigerator, standing upright, to set.

8 Place the chocolate in a bowl and microwave at 100% (high) for 1 minute to melt. Stir.

Zucchini au Gratin

9 Line a small baking sheet with foil. Spread the chocolate evenly over the foil to a depth of about ⅛ inch. Tap the sheet lightly on the work surface until the surface of the chocolate is smooth, then leave in a cool place to set.

10 Remove the chocolate from the foil. Use a heart-shaped cutter, about 1½ inches in diameter, to cut 4 hearts, then use a 1 inch cutter to cut 2 more hearts.

Leave in the refrigerator until ready to serve.

11 Whip the remaining cream until thick. Pipe a swirl on top of each glass and decorate with the chocolate hearts.

Passionfruit Creams

P·A·T·I·O S·U·P·P·E·R

Crab-Stuffed Avocados • Fish Casserole • Chocolate Cherry Cheese Pie
Serves 4

COUNTDOWN

The day before:
Make the Chocolate Cherry Cheese Pie but do not decorate. Store in the refrigerator.

45 minutes before serving:
1 Decorate the cheese pie and make the cherry sauce. Store in the refrigerator.
2 Prepare the Fish Casserole to the end of Step 3.
3 Make the Crab-Stuffed Avocados.
4 Cook the casserole while serving and eating the avocados.
5 Thicken the casserole with cornstarch, microwave at 100% (high) for 1 minute, adjust the seasoning, garnish and serve.

CRAB-STUFFED AVOCADOS

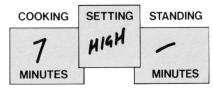

COOKING	SETTING	STANDING
7 MINUTES	HIGH	— MINUTES

2 tablespoons olive oil
1 large onion, minced
2 cloves garlic, crushed
6 oz frozen crabmeat, thawed
2 tablespoons chopped fresh parsley
1 tablespoon red or white wine vinegar
2 dashes of hot pepper sauce
¼ teaspoon salt
¼ teaspoon pepper
¼ cup grated Parmesan cheese
2 large, ripe avocados
1 tablespoon lemon juice

1 Place the oil in a 1 quart bowl, add the onion and garlic and microwave at 100% (high) for 3 minutes, stirring after 2 minutes.
2 Add the crabmeat to the onion, together with the parsley, vinegar, hot pepper sauce, salt, pepper, and half the Parmesan. Microwave at 100% (high) for 2 minutes. Stir with a wooden spoon to mix.
3 Cut the avocados in half lengthwise and remove the seeds. Brush the cut surfaces with lemon juice. Fill the avocado halves with crab mixture,

piling it up into a mound in the center and spreading it over the cut edges. Sprinkle with the remaining Parmesan.
4 Microwave at 100% (high) for 2 minutes or until the mixture is heated. Place under a preheated broiler to brown, if wished.

FISH CASSEROLE

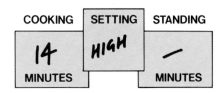

COOKING	SETTING	STANDING
14 MINUTES	HIGH	— MINUTES

2 tablespoons olive oil
2 onions, chopped
2 cloves garlic, crushed
4 scallions, chopped
1 green pepper, seeded and chopped
3 tablespoons chopped parsley
1 cup dry white wine
1 can (16 oz) chopped tomatoes
4 tablespoons tomato paste
2 tablespoons brandy (optional)
1½ lb haddock fillet, skinned and cut in 1 inch cubes
⅔ cup frozen shelled shrimp
1 tablespoon cornstarch
salt and pepper
12 cooked shrimp in shells, for garnish

1 Place the oil in a 2 quart casserole, add the onions and garlic and microwave at 100% (high) for 4 minutes, stirring once.
2 Add the scallions, green pepper and half the parsley, stir well and microwave at 100% (high) for 2 minutes.
3 Mix the wine with 2 tablespoons water and add to the casserole, together with the chopped tomatoes, tomato paste and brandy, if using. Add the haddock pieces and shelled shrimp and stir gently to mix.
4 Cover the casserole and microwave at 100% (high) for 7-8 minutes, until the haddock flakes easily when touched with a fork. Mix the cornstarch with 2 table-

spoons water, stir into the casserole and microwave at 100% (high) for 1 minute. Add salt and pepper to taste. Garnish with the shrimp in shells and serve.

CHOCOLATE CHERRY CHEESE PIE

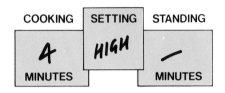

COOKING	SETTING	STANDING
4	HIGH	—
MINUTES		MINUTES

1 can (16 oz) pitted Bing cherries
3 packages (3 oz each) cream cheese
¼ cup superfine sugar
2 eggs, separated
1 tablespoon Kirsch
1 envelope unflavored gelatin
1 cup heavy cream
¼ cup light cream
3 squares (3 oz) semisweet chocolate, to decorate
1 tablespoon arrowroot
Kirsch or lemon juice, to taste
For the crust:
2 squares (2 oz) semisweet chocolate, roughly grated
¼ cup butter
2 cups chocolate wafer crumbs

1 First make the wafer crust. Grease the base of an 8 inch springform pan. In a small bowl, microwave the chocolate and butter at 100% (high) for 1-2 minutes, stirring 2-3 times, until melted. Mix with the wafer crumbs.

2 Spread the mixture evenly over the base of the pan and press down well. Chill in the refrigerator.

3 Drain the cherries, reserving the syrup. Cut the cherries in half and spread one third of them over the crumb crust.

4 In a large bowl, cream the cheese and the sugar together thoroughly. Beat in the egg yolks and Kirsch a little at a time.

5 Pour 2 tablespoons cold water into a small bowl and sprinkle over the gelatin. Leave for a few minutes to soften, then microwave at 100% (high) for 15-30 seconds to melt. Stir, then let cool slightly.

6 Mix the creams and whip the mixture until it just holds soft peaks. Beat the egg whites until they are stiff. Beat the gelatin mixture slowly into the cheese without letting lumps form. Fold in the cream, then fold in the egg whites, using a metal spoon.

7 Spoon gently onto the chilled base and spread evenly. Chill in the refrigerator for several hours, preferably overnight.

8 Shortly before serving, decorate the pie. Shave long, thin curls of chocolate off the squares with a vegetable parer or sharp knife.

9 To make the cherry sauce, mix the arrowroot to a cream with a little of the reserved syrup. Pour the remaining syrup into a bowl, adding Kirsch or lemon juice to taste. Microwave at 100% (high) for 1½-2 minutes or until boiling, then stir in the arrowroot mixture. Microwave at 100% (high) for 1 minute or until thick. Cool under a piece of dampened waxed paper.

10 Remove the cheese pie from the pan and place on a serving platter. Decorate with a ring of the remaining halved cherries. Spoon a little of the sauce over them. Arrange the chocolate around the edge of the pie and serve. Pass the rest of the sauce in a sauceboat.

Chocolate Cherry Cheese Pie

C·U·R·R·Y L·U·N·C·H

Spiced Lamb, Vegetable Curry, Beef Kheema • Black Currant Sherbet
Serves 4-6

COUNTDOWN

The day before:
1 Prepare meat and marinade and marinate the lamb for Spiced Lamb.
2 Make Black Currant Sherbet and store in the freezer.
2½ hours before serving:
1 Make Beef Kheema but do not add peas. Cover and set aside.
2 Make Spiced Lamb, cover and set aside.
3 Make Vegetable Curry and transfer to a warmed serving dish.
4 Add the peas to the Kheema and complete the recipe. Transfer to a warmed serving dish.
5 Reheat Spiced Lamb, covered, at 100% (high) for 4-5 minutes.
6 Reheat Vegetable Curry, if necessary, at 100% (high) for 1-2 minutes and garnish. Serve the curry dishes with Basmati rice, mango chutney, Raita and chopped onion and tomato.
7 Remove the sherbet from the freezer a few minutes before serving.

SPICED LAMB

COOKING	SETTING	STANDING
39 MINUTES	HIGH/MED	— MINUTES

1½ lb boneless lamb, trimmed and cut in ½ inch thick strips
2 tablespoons vegetable oil
10 whole black peppercorns
4 whole cardamom
2 cinnamon sticks
2 bay leaves
¼ teaspoon ground cloves
2 large onions, sliced
2 cloves garlic, chopped
For the marinade:
¾ cup finely ground almonds
1 tablespoon ground cumin
½ tablespoon ground ginger
1 teaspoon salt
1 cup plain yogurt
1 tablespoon lemon juice

1 To make the marinade, mix together the almonds, spices, salt, yogurt and lemon juice.
2 Put the lamb in a bowl, pour over the marinade and mix to coat well. Cover and refrigerate overnight.
3 Place the oil in a 2 quart casserole, add the peppercorns, cardamom, cinnamon sticks, bay leaves and cloves and microwave at 100% (high) for 2 minutes, stirring after 1 minute. Add the sliced onions and chopped garlic and microwave at 100% (high) for 2 minutes.
4 Add the meat and marinade, stir well, cover and microwave at 100% (high) for 5 minutes. Reduce the power to 50% (medium) and microwave for 30 minutes, stirring occasionally to ensure the meat cooks evenly.
5 Transfer the Spiced Lamb to a warmed serving dish. Serve together with the Beef Kheema and Vegetable Curry. Accompany with Basmati rice which comes from northern India and is considered to have the best flavor of all the long-grain rices. Other good accompaniments to serve with curry dishes are Raita (chopped cucumber mixed in yogurt), a salad of chopped onion and tomato, and mango chutney.

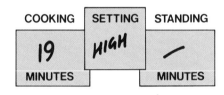

VEGETABLE CURRY

COOKING	SETTING	STANDING
19 MINUTES	HIGH	— MINUTES

2 tablespoons vegetable oil
1 tablespoon ground coriander
1 teaspoon curry powder
1 teaspoon turmeric
1 teaspoon ground cumin
1 tablespoon lemon juice
1 teaspoon salt
3 tablespoons water
2 cups raw potato chunks
1 cup frozen sliced carrots
1 cup frozen sliced zucchini
1 cup frozen green beans
2 tomatoes, quartered
fresh coriander, for garnish

1 Place the oil in a 2 quart casserole. Add the ground spices and microwave at 100% (high) for 1 minute. Add the lemon juice, salt and water.
2 Add the potatoes and carrots to the casserole and stir well so that they are coated with the

Spiced Lamb served with mango chutney, Raita, and tomato and onion salad

BEEF KHEEMA

COOKING	SETTING	STANDING
48 MINUTES	HIGH / MED	— MINUTES

2 tablespoons vegetable oil
2 tablespoons ground coriander
2 tablespoons curry powder
 or garam masala
½ tablespoon turmeric
2 onions, minced
2 cloves garlic, chopped
2 inch piece gingerroot, pared
 and chopped
1½ lb lean ground beef
2 green peppers, seeded and
 chopped
1 can (16 oz) tomatoes
1 package (10 oz) frozen peas
salt

1 Place the oil in a 2 quart casserole and stir in the ground spices, onions, garlic and ginger. Microwave at 100% (high) for 4 minutes, stirring twice.
2 Add the beef, microwave at 100% (high) for 4 minutes, breaking the meat up with a spoon 2-3 times. Stir in the green peppers, tomatoes with their juice and 3 tablespoons water.
3 Cover and microwave at 100% (high) for 5 minutes, then reduce the power to 50% (medium) for 30 minutes, stirring the mixture occasionally.
4 Stir in the peas, season with salt and cook at 100% (high) for 5 minutes. Transfer to a warmed serving dish and serve.

BLACK CURRANT SHERBET

COOKING	SETTING	STANDING
8 MINUTES	HIGH	— MINUTES

2 lb frozen black currants
2 tablespoons light corn
 syrup
1 cup superfine sugar
2 teaspoons lemon juice
1¼ cups water
2 egg whites
vanilla wafers

1 Place the black currants in a 2 quart bowl with the syrup, sugar, lemon juice and water.
2 Cover with pierced plastic wrap and microwave at 100% (high) for 8-10 minutes, or until the black currants are cooked. Stir after 5 minutes.
3 Press the cooked black currants through a strainer to remove the seeds and skins. Turn into a rigid container and freeze, uncovered, until firm around the edges.
4 Remove the black currant mixture from the freezer and break it up with a fork.
5 Beat the egg whites to stiff peaks. Fold into the black currant mixture. Cover and freeze overnight, until solid.
6 Remove the sherbet from the freezer a few minutes before it is time to serve. Scoop into individual bowls and serve with vanilla wafers.

Vegetable Curry

spice mixture. Cover and microwave at 100% (high) for 10 minutes. Add the zucchini and beans and re-cover. Microwave at 100% (high) for 6-8 minutes.
3 Stir in the tomatoes, re-cover and microwave at 100% (high) for 2 minutes. Transfer to a warmed serving dish and garnish with fresh coriander.

Black Currant Sherbet

G·R·E·E·K S·U·P·P·E·R

Pilaf, Avgolemono Lamb ●Ionian Cream
Serves 4

COUNTDOWN

In the morning:
Make the Ionian Cream, but do not invert or decorate. Store in the refrigerator.

1 hour before serving:
1 Cook the Pilaf to the end of Step 3.
2 Make the Avgolemono Lamb up to the end of Step 4.
3 While the lamb is cooking, decorate the Ionian Cream and prepare the salad for the Pilaf.
4 Prepare the Avgolemono sauce for the lamb up to the end of Step 6.
5 Reheat the rice at 100% (high) for 2 minutes while arranging the lamb on a serving dish.
6 Add the olives to the rice, press into the molds, then unmold and arrange on a plate with the salad.
7 Heat the Avgolemono sauce at 100% (high) for 30-60 seconds. Do not boil. Adjust the seasoning, if necessary, and pour over the lamb. Garnish and serve with the Pilaf and warmed pita bread, if liked.

PILAF

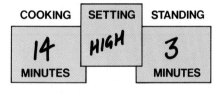

COOKING	SETTING	STANDING
14 MINUTES	HIGH	3 MINUTES

2 tablespoons margarine or
   butter
1 onion, minced
1 cup long-grain rice
2 cups hot chicken stock
1/3 cup pitted ripe olives,
   chopped
Accompaniments:
lettuce leaves
3 tomatoes, sliced
1 onion, sliced
4 pitted ripe olives

1 Place the margarine in a 2 quart bowl, add the onion and microwave at 100% (high) for 2 minutes.
2 Add the rice and stir gently. Microwave at 100% (high) for 2 minutes, until the grains are coated. Pour in the stock and stir to mix. Cover with pierced plas-

tic wrap and microwave at 100% (high) for 10 minutes, or until the rice is tender and the stock is absorbed.
3 Fork in the olives, cover and let stand for 3 minutes.
4 Press the cooked pilaf into oiled custard cups or dariole molds. Arrange the salad ingredients on a dish and invert the molds on top.

AVGOLEMONO LAMB

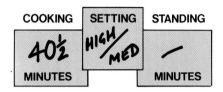

COOKING	SETTING	STANDING
40½ MINUTES	HIGH/MED	— MINUTES

2 tablespoons margarine or
   butter
1 large onion, chopped
1½ lb boneless lamb leg
   steaks, cut in 1 inch cubes
4 celery stalks, chopped
1 tablespoon chopped fresh dill
   or 1 teaspoon dried dillweed
2 cups hot vegetable stock
salt and pepper
2 small firm hearts Boston
   lettuce, cut in quarters
4 teaspoons cornstarch
2 egg yolks
2 tablespoons lemon juice
For the garnish:
2 tablespoons chopped fresh
   parsley
lemon wedges

1 Place the margarine in a 2 quart casserole. Add the onion and microwave at 100% (high) for 2 minutes. Add the lamb and microwave at 100% (high) for 5 minutes. Stir after 3 minutes.
2 Add the celery, dill and stock to the casserole and season to taste with salt and pepper. Cover and microwave at 100% (high) for 5 minutes. Reduce the power to 50% (medium) and microwave for 20 minutes.
3 Put the lettuce in a double col-

ander, pour over boiling water and drain well. Add the lettuce to the casserole, re-cover and microwave at 50% (medium) for 5 minutes.

4 Strain off the cooking liquid from the lamb into a bowl. Keep the meat and vegetables warm in the casserole.

5 To make the sauce, mix the cornstarch to a smooth paste with a little water in a small bowl. Microwave the cooking liquid in the bowl at 100% (high) for 2 minutes, or until boiling. Add the cornstarch paste, stir and microwave at 100% (high) for 1 minute, stirring frequently, until the sauce is thickened and smooth.

6 Meanwhile, beat the egg yolks in a large bowl until creamy. Beat in the lemon juice, a little at a time, until it is all incorporated. Gradually stir the hot sauce into the egg and lemon mixture in the bowl, beating well until thoroughly blended. Return the sauce to the bowl.

7 Microwave the sauce at 100% (high) for 30-60 seconds. Do not boil. Taste and adjust the seasoning if necessary.

8 Arrange the lamb and vegetables on a warmed serving dish and pour over the sauce. Garnish with the parsley and lemon wedges, serve with the Pilaf.

Ionian Cream

IONIAN CREAM

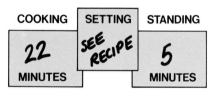

COOKING	SETTING	STANDING
22 MINUTES	*SEE RECIPE*	**5** MINUTES

1¼ cups milk
⅔ cup heavy cream
4 large eggs
3-4 drops of vanilla
¼ cup superfine sugar
For the caramel:
⅓ cup sugar
¼ cup water
To decorate:
2 apples, cored and sliced
2 oranges, peeled and sliced in rounds
a few strawberries, halved

1 For the caramel, place the sugar and water in a 3 cup bowl. Microwave at 100% (high) for 1 minute. Stir to dissolve sugar, then microwave at 100% (high) for 2-3 minutes, or until golden.

2 Pour immediately into the base of an 8-9 inch ring mold.

3 Place the milk and cream in a large measuring cup. Microwave at 100% (high) for 4-5 minutes or until it begins to bubble.

4 Beat the eggs, vanilla and sugar together in a bowl. Pour on the milk and cream mixture, beating continuously to blend. Strain over the caramel.

5 Cover with pierced plastic wrap and stand the bowl in a shallow dish. Pour enough nearly boiling water into the dish to come 2 inches up the outside of the mold.

6 Microwave at 30-50% (low-medium) for 15-20 minutes or until lightly set. Start checking after 12 minutes. Rotate the dish a quarter turn every 3 minutes.

7 Let stand for 5 minutes, then remove the mold from the water. Remove the cover and let cool.

8 Chill, then invert on a serving dish and fill the center with the mixed fruits.

S·U·M·M·E·R L·U·N·C·H

*Veal and Artichoke Casserole, Snow Peas, Italian Rice
with Almonds ● Apple Flummery – Serves 6*

COUNTDOWN

1¾ hours before serving:

1 Cook the Veal and Artichoke Casserole but do not garnish.

2 Make the Apple Flummery but do not decorate. Set in the re-frigerator until ready to serve.

3 Prepare the snow peas.

4 Cook the almonds for the Italian Rice.

5 Cook the rice and let stand for 5 minutes. While rice is standing, reheat the casserole at 100% (high) for 5 minutes. Stir once.

6 Cook the snow peas while garnishing and serving the Italian Rice and the casserole. Serve the snow peas.

7 Decorate the Apple Flummery just before serving.

SNOW PEAS

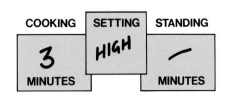

COOKING	SETTING	STANDING
3 MINUTES	HIGH	— MINUTES

¾ lb snow peas, trimmed
2 tablespoons butter
salt and pepper

1 Place the snow peas and butter in a shallow serving dish. Cover with pierced plastic wrap.
2 Microwave at 100% (high) for 3-4 minutes, stirring after 2 minutes. When cooked, snow peas should be still slightly crisp. Leave to stand, still covered, for 1-2 minutes.
3 Sprinkle with salt and pepper to taste.

VEAL & ARTICHOKE CASSEROLE

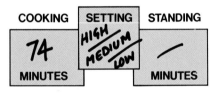

COOKING	SETTING	STANDING
74 MINUTES	HIGH MEDIUM LOW	— MINUTES

2 tablespoons margarine or
  butter
1 tablespoon olive oil
2 onions, sliced
1 clove garlic, crushed
1½ lb lean veal, cut in chunks
¾ cup medium dry white wine
1 large can (1 lb 12 oz) tomatoes
  drained and strained
2 tablespoons chopped fresh
  basil or 1 tablespoon dried
  basil
salt and pepper
1 can (16 oz) artichoke hearts,
  drained and rinsed
For the garnish:
1-2 tablespoons chopped fresh
  parsley
a little finely grated lemon rind
½ clove garlic, minced

1 Place the margarine and oil in a very large bowl or casserole. Add the onions and crushed garlic and microwave at 100% (high) for 2 minutes. Add the veal chunks and microwave at 100% (high) for a further 5 minutes, stirring twice.
2 Add the wine and microwave at 100% (high) for 10 minutes. Stir in the tomatoes, fresh or dried basil and season to taste with salt and pepper. Cover with pierced plastic wrap or a lid and microwave at 100% (high) for 7-8 minutes. Reduce the power to 50% (medium) and microwave for a further 20 minutes.
3 Stir in the artichokes, and microwave at 30% (low) for 30-40 minutes.
4 Transfer the casserole to a serving dish if necessary. Mix together the chopped parsley, grated lemon rind and minced garlic and sprinkle over the casserole before serving.

ITALIAN RICE WITH ALMONDS

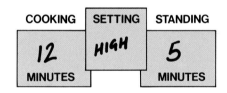

COOKING	SETTING	STANDING
12 MINUTES	HIGH	5 MINUTES

1⅓ cups long-grain rice
salt
1 tablespoon olive oil
¼ cup slivered almonds

1 Place the rice in a large deep bowl. Add 3 cups boiling water, season to taste with salt and add the olive oil.
2 Cover with pierced plastic wrap and microwave at 100% (high) for 12 minutes. Let stand for 5 minutes.
3 Toast the almonds (see Microtip, page 93).
4 Place the rice on a warmed serving dish and sprinkle with the toasted almonds.

APPLE FLUMMERY

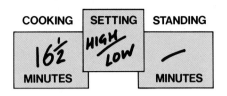

COOKING	SETTING	STANDING
16½ MINUTES	HIGH LOW	— MINUTES

2 large eggs, separated
3 tablespoons sugar
2½ cups milk
⅓ cup semolina flour
pinch of salt
10 oz pared and cored
  cooking apples
juice of ½ lemon
To serve:
6 vanilla wafers
1 red-skinned apple
a few drops of lemon juice

1 Put the egg yolks and sugar in a bowl and beat together until creamy.
2 Put the milk into a 1 quart bowl and microwave at 100% (high) for 3 minutes. Sprinkle in the semolina flour and stir. Microwave at 100% (high) for 2½-3 minutes, or until boiling, stirring 3-4 times.
3 Cover with pierced plastic wrap and microwave at 30% (low) for 10 minutes, stirring every 3-4 minutes.
4 Gradually stir in the egg yolk and sugar mixture until well mixed, then microwave at 100% (high) for 1 minute.
5 Meanwhile, purée the apple in a blender or food processor with the lemon juice. Place the purée in a large bowl and stir in the semolina mixture.
6 Beat the egg whites until stiff and fold into the mixture, using a metal spoon. Carefully spoon into 6 serving glasses and let cool for about 30 minutes.
7 To serve, thinly slice the red apple, discarding the core, but leaving the skin on. Sprinkle immediately with lemon juice to prevent discoloration. Decorate each glass with cookies and apple slices before serving.

Apple Flummery

H·A·N·D·Y C·O·O·K·E·R·Y C·H·A·R·T

GUIDE TO COOKING FRESH AND FROZEN FOODS IN A MICROWAVE OVEN

(All microwave ovens vary slightly and you may need to to adjust the timing. These charts are all based upon an oven with an output of 700 watts and times are for cooking at 100% (high) unless otherwise stated.)

FOODS	QUANTITY	COOKING* (mins)	STANDING (mins)	SPECIAL INSTRUCTIONS
Apples, *baked*	4 medium	8-10	2-3	Arrange apples in circle. Cover with pierced plastic wrap.
stewed	1 lb	6-8	2	Cover tightly. Stir halfway through cooking.
Bacon, *slices*	1	1	—	Lay between sheets of paper towels on a plate or roasting rack.
Beans, *Green or Wax*				
fresh	1 lb	8-10	2-3	Add 2 tablespoons water. Stir once or twice. Add salt after cooking.
frozen	10 oz pkg	6-8	3	As above.
Lima, fresh	1 lb	9-11	2-3	As above.
frozen	10 oz pkg	7-8	3	As above.
Beef, *boned roast*	per lb	6-7 (rare)	10-15	Stand roast on roasting rack. Cover with paper towels.
		7-8 (med)	10-15	Turn halfway through cooking.
		8½-10 (well done)	15-20	
steaks (¾ inch thick)	1 lb	5-7	5	Cook on roasting rack, uncovered. Turn over once.
Blackberries, blueberries, Black Currants etc.	1 lb	3-4	2	Add 1-2 tablespoons water. Sweeten to taste. Stir once during cooking.
Broccoli, fresh	1 lb	8-10	3-4	Place heads toward center of dish. Add 2-3 tablespoons water. Rearrange after 4 minutes.
frozen	10 oz pkg	8-10	3-4	Break apart as soon as possible and rearrange halfway through cooking.
Brussels sprouts,				
fresh	1 lb	8-10	2-3	Add 2 tablespoons water. Stir once or twice during cooking.
frozen	10 oz pkg	6-7	3	As above.
Cabbage, *shredded*	1 lb	9-11	2-3	Add 2-3 tablespoons water. Stir once or twice during cooking.
Carrots, *sliced*				
fresh	½ lb	7-8	2	Add 2 tablespoons water. Stir once or twice during cooking.
frozen chunks	10 oz pkg	7-8	3	As above.
Cauliflower, *flowerets*				
fresh	1 lb	9-11	3-5	Place heads toward center of dish. Add 2-3 tablespoons water. Rearrange after 5 minutes.
frozen	10 oz package	6-7	3	Place in a shallow dish. Add ⅓ cup water. Cover with pierced plastic wrap. Rearrange halfway through cooking.
Chicken, *whole*	per lb	8 at 70% (medium high)	10-15	Stand breast-down on roasting rack. Cover. Turn halfway through cooking.
portions	4	8-9 at 70% (medium high)	10	Arrange in dish. Turn over and rearrange halfway through cooking. Frozen chicken must be completely thawed before cooking.
Corn *whole kernels* frozen	10 oz pkg	5-7	2	Add 1 tablespoon water and knob of butter. Cover. Stir once or twice during cooking.
corn-on-the-cob (thawed or fresh)	2	6-7	3	Wrap in buttered waxed paper. Turn over once or twice during cooking.
Eggs, *baked*	2	2¼ at 50% (medium)	1	Prepare in usual way. Prick yolks with cocktail pick. Cover with pierced plastic wrap.
poached	2	1	1-2	Break eggs into 1 cup boiling water with 1 teaspoon vinegar added. Prick yolks and cover. Do not overcook.
scrambled	2	1½	1	Melt a knob of butter. Add 2 tablespoons milk. Beat in eggs. Stir in 30 seconds
Fish fillets, *white*	1 lb	5-7	2-3	Arrange with thinner parts to center of dish. Cover tightly Rearrange carefully after 3 mins.
Fish sticks, frozen	6	3	—	Place on plate. Cover with pierced plastic wrap. Rearrange once during cooking.
Gooseberries	1 lb	3-4	1	Add ¼ cup water. Sweeten. Cover. Stir gently twice during cooking.
Hamburgers, fresh	2 x ¼ lb	3-3½	1-2	Put on a roasting rack. Cover with paper towels. Cook 1½ mins. Turn over and cook to desired doneness.
frozen	4 x 2 oz	3-4	1-2	As above, or cook in preheated browning dish. Separate as soon as possible and turn over halfway through cooking.

FOODS	QUANTITY	COOKING* (mins)	STANDING (mins)	SPECIAL INSTRUCTIONS
Lamb, *roast, bone-in*	per l lb	11 at 70% (medium high)	15-20	Stand on roasting rack. Shield bone end with thin strip of foil if allowed. Cover with absorbent kitchen paper. Turn over halfway through cooking.
chops	4 large	12 at 70% (medium high)	5	Cook on roasting rack. Cover with paper towels. Turn over and rearrange halfway through cooking.
Leeks, *sliced*	1 lb	8-10	2-3	Add 2 tablespoons water and knob of butter. Stir once or twice during cooking.
Meat, *ground*	1 lb	7-8	2-3	Break up in dish. Drain off fat after 4 minutes and stir well.
Mixed vegetables, *frozen*	10 oz pkg	5-7	2	Add 1-2 tablespoons water. Stir once or twice during cooking.
Mushrooms, *whole*	½ lb	3-4	1-2	Put in dish with 2 tablespoons butter. Stir twice during cooking.
Onions, *small whole*	½ lb	3-4	—	Place in a shallow dish and cover with pierced plastic wrap. Rearrange halfway through cooking.
Pasta	6 oz	12-15 at 30% (low)	5	Add 3 quarts boiling salted water. Cook at 100% (high) until water reboils, then switch to 30% (low). Stir once or twice during cooking.
Peas, *fresh*	1 lb	6-8	2	Add 2 tablespoons water and sprig of mint. Stir once or twice during cooking.
frozen	10 oz pkg.	5-7	2	As above.
Plums	1 lb	3-4	2	Add 3-4 tablespoons water. Sweeten to taste. Cover. Stir once or twice during cooking.
Pork, *roast, bone-in*	1 lb	12 at 70% (medium high)	15-20	Rub rind with oil and salt. Stand rind-down on roasting rack. Cover loosely with paper towels. Turn over halfway through cooking. Cover bone end with thin strip of foil if allowed.
chops	2 large	15 at 50% (medium)	10	Stand on roasting rack. Turn over and rearrange halfway through cooking.
Potatoes, *boiled*	1 lb	8-10	3	Cut in even-size pieces. Add 2 tablespoons water. Stir once or twice during cooking.
jacket	1 x 6 oz	4	5	Scrub, prick, wrap in paper towels. Turn over halfway through cooking.
Pouch meals, *frozen*	1 portion	3½	2	Slit top of bag. Place on plate. Shake gently halfway through cooking.
Rhubarb, *cut in 1 inch pieces*	1 lb	6-8	2-3	Add 1 tablespoon water and sugar to taste. Stir gently halfway through cooking.
Rice, *long-grain*	1 cup	5 at 100% (high then 12 at 50% (medium)		Mix rice with 1¾ cups boiling salted water in a large dish. Cover with loose-fitting lid.
brown	1 cup	5 at 100% (high) then 25 at 50% (medium)	5	As above.
Sausage links	1 lb	13	5-10	Cook in a preheated browning dish, turning once or twice during cooking.
Smoked fish fillets	1 lb	4-5	2-3	Arrange with thinner parts toward center of dish. Add 1 tablespoon milk or water. Cover tightly. Carefully rearrange halfway through cooking.
Spinach, *fresh*	1 lb	6-8	2	Do not add water. Cover tightly. Stir once or twice during cooking.
frozen	10 oz	6-8	2	As above.
Tomatoes, *halved*	½ lb	3-4	2-3	Stand in a ring on a plate. Do not add water. Cover with waxed paper. Rearrange halfway through cooking.
Trout, Salmon Herring etc. *whole*	per 1 lb	6-7	2-3	Cover heads and tails with thin strips of foil, if allowed. Wrap in buttered waxed paper
Turkey	per 1 lb	6-8	15-20	Best results if cooked at 50% (medium) for second half of cooking. Treat as for chicken. Frozen turkey must be completely thawed before cooking.
Turnip and Rutabaga *diced*	1 lb	6-8	3	Add 2 tablespoons water, stir once or twice during cooking.

I·N·D·E·X